W9-ASJ-597

TWAYNE'S WORLD AUTHORS SERIES

A Survey of the World's Literature

SPAIN

Calderón de la Barca

(*TWAS 30*)

TWAYNE'S WORLD AUTHORS SERIES (TWAS)

The purpose of TWAS is to survey the major writers —novelists, dramatists, historians, poets, philosophers, and critics—of the nations of the world. Among the national literatures covered are those of Australia, Canada, China, Eastern Europe, France, Germany, Greece, India, Italy, Japan, Latin America, New Zealand, Poland, Russia, Scandinavia, Spain, and the African nations, as well as Hebrew, Yiddish, and Latin Classical literatures. This survey is complemented by Twayne's United States Authors Series and English Authors Series

The intent of each volume in these series is to present a critical-analytical study of the works of the writer; to include biographical and historical material that may be necessary for understanding, appreciation, and critical appraisal of the writer; and to present all material in clear, concise English—but not to vitiate the scholarly content of the work by doing so.

Calderón de la Barca

By EVERETT W. HESSE
University of Southern California

Twayne Publishers, Inc. :: New York

Library of Congress Catalog Card Number: 67–25182

MANUFACTURED IN THE UNITED STATES OF AMERICA

TO

GERALD E. WADE

In Grateful Appreciation

What is life? A frenzy.
What is life? An illusion,
a shadow, a fiction,
and the greatest good is small;
for all life is like a dream,
and dreams are nothing more than dreams.
(*Life is a Dream,* Act II)

¿Qué es la vida? Un frenesí,
¿Qué es la vida? Una ilusión,
una sombra, una ficción,
y el mayor bien es pequeño;
que toda la vida es sueño,
y los sueños sueños son
(*La vida es sueño,* Act II)

Preface

This study of Don Pedro Calderón de la Barca proposes to give the reader some understanding and appreciation of the dramatic art and genius of one of Spain's great playwrights of the seventeenth century. Because he lived over three hundred years ago in an age quite different from ours, because his expression is often so condensed and so imaginative, Calderón needs considerable annotation and interpretation if he is to be understood and appreciated by the modern reader. Therefore, I include in the Chronology the most important events in his life; in Chapters 1–4 I provide background information regarding the times of Calderón, the development of the national theater, the rise of the *comedia,* and a brief account of his dramatic and poetic art. In Chapters 12–13 I offer a survey of his minor works, and an overview of his theater by the critics.

In Chapters 5–11 I present a brief summary of the salient features of his theater, the names of representative plays and a critical analysis in some detail of one or more important plays in each classification rather than a superficial treatment of all. Since Calderón has left a dramatic legacy of some one hundred ten plays, the limitations of space will permit the discussion in depth of only the following plays: *The House with Two Doors* (*Casa con dos puertas*); *The Mayor of Zalamea* (*El alcalde de Zalamea*); *Absalom's Hair* (*Los cabellos de Absalón*), *The Constant Prince* (*El príncipe constante*), *The Wonder-Working Magician* (*El mágico prodigioso*); *Daughter of the Air* (*La hija del aire*); *The Greatest Monster, Jealousy* (*El mayor monstruo, los celos*), *The Physician of His Honor* (*El médico de su honra*); *Prometheus' Statue* (*La estatua de Prometeo*), *Echo and Narcissus* (*Eco y Narciso*); *Life is a Dream* (*La vida es sueño*); *and The Great Theater of the World* (*El gran teatro del mundo*).

The prose translations are my free renditions of the original Spanish. One of the greatest hindrances to an understanding and appreciation of Calderón's theater by those who do not read Spanish is the paucity of satisfactory translations beyond a half dozen or so for the best known plays. For years the emasculated versions of Edward Fitzgerald have provided the general public with a distorted, false impression of Calderón's genius. It is only in recent years that an attempt has been made to correct this unfortunate situation by rendering more exact and more poetic translations into English.

The Selected Bibliography is divided into the following categories: Early Volumes of Plays, Three Modern Collections, Editions of the *Autos Sacramentales;* Biography and Bibliography; General Studies on Calderón; Studies on Individual Plays; English Translations of Plays and *Autos;* Studies on the *Autos Sacramentales;* The Age of Calderón; The Question of Honor; Dramatic Theory; and Studies on Golden Age Drama and Theater. I have given only some of the most important items of general interest plus a few of the more technical ones for the curious reader who may wish to pursue further study in depth.

Finally, I wish to acknowledge a deep sense of gratitude to those authors and critics mentioned in the Notes to the Chapters and in the Selected Bibliography whose studies have been a beacon illuminating my way, among them Alexander A. Parker, Albert E. Sloman, Angel Valbuena Briones, Angel Valbuena Prat, Bruce W. Wardropper, William M. Whitby and Edward M. Wilson. I should also like to thank Professor Gerald E. Wade for his constant encouragement in the preparation of this volume.

E.W.H.

Los Angeles, Calif.

Contents

study of Pec
its critical ove
cy left by one
of her Golden Age
ern reader to gai
eciation of Calde
ssor Hesse ex-
the plays, and
and themes.
ely analyzed
interpretations
onsideration of

Chronology

1600 Pedro Calderón de la Barca born January 17; baptized February 14.

1608– Attended the Colegio Imperial, a Jesuit school in Ma-
1613 drid.

1614– Divided his time between the University of Alcalá and the
1620 University of Salamanca where he received a degree in canonical law, which along with theology, scholastic philosophy and logic was his favorite subject. The influence of these disciplines is most evident in his plays where they appear in the form of argumentation and reasoning even in matters of love.

1620– Participated in poetic contests in honor of the beatification
1622 and canonization of St. Isadore, patron saint of Madrid. Praised by Lope de Vega.

1623 His first play, *Love, Honor and Power* (*Amor, honor y poder*), performed in Madrid.

1623– Probably saw military service in Italy and Flanders. May
1625 have participated in the surrender of Breda, the subject of his play, *The Siege of Breda* (*El sitio de Breda*), performed in 1625, the theme of Velázquez' picture, *The Lances,* painted in 1635.

1630– Years of his most productive dramatic output.
1650

1634 Opening of the court theater, *El Coliseo del Buen Retiro.*

1635 Becomes court dramatist after the death of Lope de Vega.

1636 Publication of the *First Part* of his dramas (12 plays).

1636– Received appointment to the coveted Order of Santiago.
1637

1637 Publication of the *Second Part* (12 plays).

1640– Journeyed to Catalonia with his Order to suppress the re-
1641 bellion.

1642 Ill health forces him to return to Madrid.
1651 Ordained a priest, following the death of his two brothers and a mistress. Becomes private chaplain to the King. Limits his literary activity to writing plays for the court and religious pieces for the Municipality of Madrid.
1664 Publication of his *Third Part* (12 plays).
1672 Publication of his *Fourth Part* (12 plays).
1677 The "unauthorized" *Fifth Part* (of the 10 plays, he disowns four).
1681 Died May 25.

CHAPTER 1

The Age of Calderón

CALDERÓN'S life extended over almost the complete reign of two monarchs, Philip III (1598–1621), and Philip IV (1621–1665), and it also covered that of most of a third, Charles II (1665–1700). The greater part of it fell in the epoch of Philip IV, often called Felipe el Grande, the king in whose reign the arts and literature reached their zenith.

I *The Political Climate*

The personal rule of monarchs like Charles I (also called Charles V in his role of Holy Roman Emperor) and his son Philip II, who between them reigned most of the sixteenth century, now gave way to rule by royal favorites. The kings of the seventeenth century no longer took a personal interest in the affairs of state. The Duke of Lerma and his son the Duke of Uceda held the reins of government under Philip III. Olivares, of whom Velázquez has left a masterful portrait, kept the monarch's attention from affairs of state by entertaining him with all sorts of diversions, soirées, and expensive theatrical performances.

During the seventeenth century Spain not only suffered the piece-meal disintegration of its far-flung empire through foreign wars, but also had to contend with revolts at home, notably in Catalonia and Portugal in 1640. Calderón in the *Mayor of Zalamea* (*El alcalde de Zalamea*), the action of which took place in 1580, dealt with that aspect of the revolts which aimed to expose the irresponsible conduct of Spanish troops billeted in the homes of the civilian population.

II *The Social-Economic Situation*

The decline which had already begun with the destruction of the Spanish Armada in 1588 was to be observed in almost every phase of life. The great majority of Spaniards who had any pretension to nobility (real or imaginary) shunned manual labor, industry, commerce, banking, and farming; in their false pride they considered such tasks degrading and below their dignity. Young men seeking a career in life entered law, the church, or the armed forces. Furthermore, there was always the glittering court where those with influence could obtain royal favors and sinecures. As a consequence, Madrid was thronged with office-seekers, soldiers-of-fortune, parasites, rogues, thieves and vagabonds. The legal profession was overcrowded, and swarms of religious swelled the ranks of those not gainfully employed. Those Jews who had not been expelled in 1492, Moriscos (Moors converted to Christianity), and foreigners controlled much of the wealth and performed most of the work of the nation.

The flow of silver and gold that poured in from the New World paid for foreign wars, and also for the pomp, ceremony and entertainment of an extravagant court. A gyrating spiral of inflation gripped the country largely because of the debasement of the coinage in a futile effort to stave off national bankruptcy. The peasantry groaned under a crushing burden of sales taxes, miscellaneous imposts and the government monopoly on various commodities. A further cause of economic decline was the expense of an excessive number of civil servants on the government payroll.

Calderón makes little or no mention of the wretched social and economic conditions of the times, nor of the misery of the poor. His one gesture toward the recognition of the national decadence was his presentation of the impoverished nobleman of *The Mayor of Zalamea.*

III *The Religious Atmosphere*

The Church continued to play a large part in national life. It was represented at all levels and functions of government; the King, for example, was served by a personal chaplain. It exacted tithes, first fruits, and other revenues. The Inquisition sought to stamp out heresy and prevent converts from returning to previous non-Catholic practices. Convents and monasteries multiplied and accumulated great wealth and much land.

Calderón has been called a Catholic poet. During much of his life he lived in a kind of dream-world at the court where all his needs were satisfied. His religious plays are more concerned with theological problems, saints' lives, apparitions of the Virgin, and stories from the Bible than with social and economic problems. But when he deals with problems of personal philosophy he produces a masterpiece like *Life is a Dream.* He can also approach men's problems from a philosophical, moral and religious point of view as he has done so successfully in *The Great Theater of the World* (to be discussed in our Chapter X).

IV *The Palace Scene*

In the early thirties the Prime Minister and favorite, Olivares, conceived the idea of constructing a new palace since the old Alcázar was too somber and unsuited for the joyous life he believed the monarch should lead. It was a large part of Calderón's task as a member of the court to help keep the royal circle entertained. And so when the new palace was finished in 1634, he wrote as a part of the celebration of its completion an *auto sacramental* (a one-act religious piece dealing with the Eucharist) entitled *The New Palace of the Retiro* (*El Nuevo Palacio del Retiro*). The following year *Love, the Greatest Enchanter* (*El mayor encanto, amor*) had its première there on an island in the lagoons of the formal gardens. The King and his retainers were watching the performance from gondolas when a sudden windstorm upset the boats and extinguished the lights.

It was after the death of Lope de Vega in 1635 that Calderón became the official court dramatist to Philip IV. In this capacity he was called on to compose plays for such special occasions as the Queen's birthday, the arrival of visiting royalty, and the birth of an heir to the throne. Just as Velázquez was the court painter who has left for posterity portraits of Philip, his family and his retinue, so Calderón, the official court playwright, has given us a legacy of verbal cameos of the persons and places associated with the court of Philip IV.

After 1651 when Calderón became a priest, he limited his literary activity to two *autos sacramentales* a year for the city of Madrid, and to lavish court spectacles based usually on a mythological story and accompanied by elaborate stage machinery, ornate sets, gorgeous costumes, intricate lighting effects and music. Cosme Lotti and other designers of stage effects were imported from Italy to supervise the technical aspects of theatrical performances.

V *The Artistic Milieu*

During Calderón's lifetime Spanish painting reached glorious heights. While Calderón was still a youth, he must have viewed the elongated and distorted mystical figures of El Greco (1548–1625). In his later years he probably saw the sweet-faced madonnas and cherubs of another great Spanish artist, Murillo (1617–1682), whose Immaculate Conceptions adorned church buildings. But in Spanish art the name of Velázquez (1599–1660) towers above all others. Early recognizing the latent genius of the budding young artist, Olivares invited him to Madrid where he won the favor of Philip and was given a studio in the palace which the King visited almost daily. Velázquez has left us a large gallery of royal portraits: Philip IV, his first wife Isabel, Mariana, his second wife, Prince Baltasar Carlos and Princess Margarita, as well as ladies-in-waiting, gentlemen, dwarfs and buffoons of the court whom Calderón mentions by name in his plays and *zarzuelas* (See Chapter XI on the *Zarzuelas*). Perhaps his best-known historical work is "The Surrender of Breda" (1635), more popularly called "The Lances." It bears a close affinity to Calderón's play on the same subject.[1]

When Calderón began writing for the theater, the dramatic formula had already been moulded. His predecessor, Lope de Vega (1562–1635), had developed what came to be called the *comedia* ("drama" rather than "comedy"), a three-act play in verse. In his *The New Art of Play Writing* (*El arte nuevo de hacer comedias,* 1609), Lope set forth some rules for composing plays. The first act is to concern itself with explanation, the second with complication and the third with the resolution of the plot, but the dénouement is left to the last scene to discourage the spectators from vacating the theater before the play ends.

Whereas Lope composed plays with such rapidity that he is often charged with careless writing and technical flaws, Calderón was more careful in the craftsmanship of his plays and more polished in his verse forms. Calderón inherited the magic formula from Lope which he imitated with great success, embellishing his dramatic poetry with a profusion of rhetorical figures and sensuous images. In fact Calderón developed a mannerism in writing that is often compared with the manneristic style found in the painters of that era.

Lope enjoyed a popular favor that made him the envy of his literary colleagues. From his fertile pen flowed perhaps as many as 1500 dramas of which about 450 have been preserved. Some of his best known are *The Sheep's Well* (*Fuente ovejuna*), *The Scatterbrain* (*La dama boba*), *The Gentleman from Olmedo* (*El caballero de Olmedo*) and *Peribáñez.*

Another of Calderón's contemporaries was Gabriel Téllez, better known by his pseudonym Tirso de Molina (1580–1648), whose play *The Deceiver of Seville* (*El burlador de Sevilla*) deals with the Don Juan theme.

Along with Lope, Tirso and Calderón, the fourth great dramatist of the day was the Mexican-born hunchback, Juan Ruiz de Alarcón (1581–1639) whose ethical plays *Suspicious Truth* (La *verdad sospechosa*) and *The Walls have Ears* (*Las paredes oyen*), are among his best known.

Calderón's plays include much Gongorism and conceptism. The term Gongorism (*gongorismo*), which derives from the name of the leading poet of the era, Góngora, means a deliberate ornamentation and obscurity of style through the excessive use of mythological allusions, archaic words and neologisms, hyperboles and their accumulation, a highly Latinized syntax, rhetorical devices and figures of speech and a general striving for effect.[2] Conceptism (*conceptismo*), found chiefly in prose, refers to cultivated subtlety, play on words, and the use of dialectics and casuistry. Quevedo and Gracián were the principal cultivators of conceptism. It has been customary to differentiate *conceptismo* from *culteranismo* (or *gongorismo*) by stating that the former deals with ideas and the latter with words. There is considerable overlapping and there is now a tendency to include both under the term "baroque." As stated, Calderón drew heavily upon the two.

However, he could not indulge in the obscurity of a Góngora with all its contorted syntax, wealth of mythological allusion and ramification of meaning without suffering the loss of his audience. While he sprinkled his plays with sufficient Gongorism to make them conform to the vogue of the day, he was still able to attain wide popularity. Nowadays, however, the reader requires a heavily annotated edition to understand and appreciate some of the mythological and historical allusions found in several of his plays.

CHAPTER 2

The Comedia

I *The Evolution of the* Comedia

THE *comedia* may be defined as a three-act play in verse that developed and flourished in Spain during the latter part of the sixteenth century as well as all of the seventeenth century. Its form and spirit were the creation of Lope de Vega, that "monster of nature," as Cervantes called him. We will now trace the development of the Spanish theater down the centuries to see what the *comedia* extracted from its predecessors.[1]

The Play of the Magi Kings (*El auto de los Reyes Magos*) is the oldest dramatic work in Spanish literature, dating from the end of the twelfth or beginning of the thirteenth century. Of unknown authorship, it recounts the Biblical story of the visit of the Magi Kings to Jerusalem at the time of Christ's birth. It was composed for the feast of the Epiphany and was enacted in church by members of the clergy for the edification and instruction of the congregation. The unique manuscript containing one hundred forty-seven lines is written in a variety of verse forms. It has elements which will show up again later in the *comedia:* the inner conflict of one or more characters, rapidity of action and movement, naturalness of dialogue, realism of character portrayal, the dramatic soliloquy, an attempt to utilize verse forms suitable to the action.

Juan del Encina (1468?–1529?) is often called the father of the Spanish theater, for he took the drama out of the church (and churchyard) and performed it in the castles and palaces of the nobles. His early dramatic production consisted of *Eclogues* written in imitation of Vergil's, which he translated. Encina's realistic shepherds spoke in local dialect called *sayagués,* which takes its name from Sayago, a community near Zamora. Encina was fond of music which he injected into his plays and, in a sense, he anticipated the later development of the musical comedy (*zarzuela*).

He is also considered a forerunner of the short skit, the *entremés*.

Bartolomé de Torres Naharro (1476?–1531?) was the first playwright to etch typical Spanish characters. He was also noted for his rules for dramatic composition set forth in the Prologue to his *Propaladia* (*The First Fruits of Pallas,* Greek goddess of the intellect, and by extension Torres' own genius) and six plays with two more added in later editions.

Torres' main ideas on drama may be summarized as follows:

1. Plays should consist of five acts, called *jornadas,* a term often used throughout the seventeenth century to mean "acts."
2. Comedy and tragedy should be separate.
3. The number of characters should be between six and twelve.
4. Plays should be categorized as a) imaginary, consisting of an imaginative action with a semblance of reality; and b) realistic, consisting of truly factual events.
5. Decorum and verisimilitude should be observed; dialogue should be appropriate to the character.

Torres followed in the footsteps of Juan del Encina whom he probably knew in Rome. He is important for producing a comedy of intrigue which became widespread in the seventeenth century. He also essayed the honor theme and authored the first "Cape and Sword" play in what is usually considered his masterpiece, *The Play about Himenea* (*Comedia Himenea*).

Lope de Rueda (1510?–1565), a native of Seville, became a manager, actor and playwright. With a traveling company of players, he barnstormed all over Spain and thus democratized the drama, bringing it to people in all walks of life, and performing also in the palaces of the nobility, in theaters, plazas and on street corners.

In imitation of Plautus and the Italian playwrights of the Renaissance, Rueda wrote five long plays. In addition, he has left about forty short farces called *pasos*. The plot is slight, usually based on some episode from real life, and its only purpose was to amuse. These compositions were brief and were often performed as a prologue to or between the acts of a longer play. The dialogue and the situations were all-important.

Rueda's ten *pasos* show the influence of the Italian *commedia dell' arte* an improvised sort of farce then being played in Spain. His best skit, *The Olives* (*Las aceitunas*), 1548, is based on an argument between husband and wife over the price of olives which they hope to get when the trees, that have just been planted, will bear.

Juan de la Cueva (1550?–1610?), also a native of Seville, based his plays on epic poems, legends, chronicles and ballads. He explained his dramatic doctrines in his *Exemplar poético,* 1600; they may be summarized thus:

1. Reduction in the number of acts from five to four.
2. Disregard of the three unities of time, place and action.
3. Greater use of national themes.
4. More metrical variety.
5. Mixture of comedy and tragedy.
6. Intervention of royalty on the stage.
7. Utilization of the fantastic and the supernatural.

Of his fourteen plays, *The Seven Princes of Lara* (*Los siete infantes de Lara*), 1579, is a re-working of the well-known legend.

Cueva's importance lies in his emphasis on themes and situations from Spain's historical past. Lope de Vega followed Cueva in his extensive use of historical themes for his plays.

Miguel de Cervantes Saavedra (1547–1616), better known for his *Don Quijote,* the *Exemplary Novels* and his *Interludes,* is also the author of eight long plays. He favored the classic concept of playwriting, but his genius did not lie in that direction. His best known play is *La Numancia,* in four acts. It treats of the siege of the town of Numantia by some eighty thousand Roman soldiers under the leadership of Scipio Africanus. The play has been much admired and produced down the centuries because of its inspiring treatment of the theme of freedom. Its importance to the development of the *comedia* is its mingling of idealistic and realistic scenes, of allegorical figures as well as characters of flesh and blood.

Cervantes excels, however, in his eight *Interludes,* reminiscent of the farces of Lope de Rueda. They contain vivid dialogue, a slight plot, little or no character portrayal. They are a realistic reflection of the customs of the day. Like the skits of Lope de Rueda, the interludes were intended for presentation between the acts of a longer play. They continued a tradition which has lasted to the present. One of his best is *The Cave of Salamanca* (*La cueva de Salamanca*). An old husband, Pancracio, is called out of town and must leave his young wife. During his absence we learn that her tears were all feigned and that her maid has arranged with the village priest and barber to keep them company. A vagrant student asks for lodging and is permitted to stay. The husband returns home unexpectedly and the suitors must hide. The clever student, showing off the secrets he has learned in the Cave of Salamanca, produces two devils in the forms of the village priest and barber. The husband is duly impressed and the interlude ends on a note of merriment.

II *The Magnetic Pull of the* Comedia

The *comedia* became so popular that people stayed away from work to attend a performance. In fact, morning representations were finally forbidden and no theater was permitted to open its doors before noon. Women were no less avid theater-goers than men and on one occasion several hundred women surged into the theater to see a performance. The number of companies increased and included several which operated without the King's license. How explain the magnetic drawing power of the *comedia*? [2]

First, it provided a means of escape from the cares and toil of everyday life. For those Spaniards who could not travel to the New World and other distant points, there were plays dealing with adventures in far off places that appealed to the imagination.

Second, it exalted the monarchy and the national traditions. The King was depicted as the champion of the people against powerful and vindictive "nobles," who sought to foist their will on others. It upheld the dignity and decorum of women by rarely presenting a mother on the stage; unmarried women were usually accompanied by a servant, an esquire or some member of the family. It exalted the role of the Church in spreading Christianity, explaining doctrine and increasing veneration of the Virgin, all of which had been part and parcel of Spanish life down the centuries.

Third, it presented burning questions of honor which tugged at the audience's heart strings. The slaying of an innocent female victim merely suspected of infidelity became the theme of such memorable plays as Calderón's *The Physician of his Honor* (*El médico de su honra*), to be discussed later.

Fourth, it provided amusement by presenting a character who

finds himself in an awkward situation because of his own doing, or because of mistaken identity, cross purposes, or his lack of understanding of a problem. Then again, the clown (*gracioso*) found his way even into serious plays for comic relief.

Fifth, the *comedia* almost always dealt with a love affair of one sort or another. Matters of the heart have captivated mankind down the centuries. The love affair often turned into a clever game, pitting a scheming female against an unsuspecting but ardent male.

Sixth, the *comedia* appealed to the patriotism of the Spaniards. National heroes dashed across the boards in battles with their enemies whom they defeated to the entire satisfaction of the audience.

The *comedia* above all is action. In the successful plays, there is never a dull moment: battles, disputes, murders, earthquakes and other cataclysmic manifestations of nature. The *comedia* is also conflict. It pits good against evil in many ways: the overbearing noble versus the peasant, Christians against Moors, Spaniards versus Flemings, father versus son, and finally man against himself.

III *The Importance of the* Comedia

The Spanish *comedia* of the seventeenth century now occupies an admired place in world theater behind Shakespeare and the Elizabethan dramatists, and the masters of the Greek Classical Theater. In bulk alone it exceeded the output of all the Elizabethan playwrights. In fact Lope de Vega is often credited with about 1,500 plays of which some four hundred sixty have been preserved. By the year 1630, over sixty dramatists were active in Castile alone. The great abundance of printed editions of *comedias* in the seventeenth century and the publication of many individual plays throughout the eighteenth bear witness to the large reading public which sprang up during those centuries and avidly read the works of Golden Age dramatists.

The sixteenth and seventeenth centuries of Spain are commonly thought of as the Golden Centuries of its civilization. During these two hundred years the Spanish genius came to fruition in all endeavors of artistic expression suited to it, not to mention the flowering of political, religious and military achievements. Perhaps of all the multifold genres of national and universal aesthetic expression which flourished, the *comedia* evolved into the most varied and distinctive form of human articulation in the peninsula. The theater became the pulse and barometer of Spanish life, reflecting Spanish temperament and sensibilities in all their phases. The *comedia,* then, represents one of the high points of peninsular creative effort at a time when Spanish power, culture and influence enjoyed their maximum prestige. Yet today a theater so vitally expressive of the greatest power on earth at that time is little known outside the area of Spanish studies and sometimes misunderstood by those who profess to be experts in it.

Spanish drama has no Shakespeare—but neither does that of any other nation. Yet Racine, Corneille and Ibsen are well known; the same cannot be said of Lope, Tirso and Calderón, to mention only the "big three." Perhaps the most central factor of all is the notion that Spain's Golden Age theater expresses only the superficial through an elaborate stage action. Therefore, why should this theater merit translation into other languages? The question we must ask ourselves is: what has the *comedia* to offer? Is it a mere presentation of a highly concentrated action depicting nothing more than a surface reflection of Spanish daily life of the seventeenth century? If it represents nothing more than this, why should anyone wish to study a theater which provides only a one-dimensional sketch of life? Why should anyone emphasize an art form which promises little of enduring human value and transcendent experience? Or, does the *comedia* offer more in terms of human values and aesthetic merits than has hitherto been studied?

In any attempt to fathom the profundity and expressiveness of the *comedia,* one must first abandon the notion that, due to the exorbitant demand for theatrical performances in the seventeenth century, the dramatist could do no more than dash off a hastily constructed play with little or no human depth. Research in the *comedia* during the last thirty years has more than demonstrated the significance and artistic worth of the genre. During the 1930's, British Hispanists were in the vanguard of the revaluation of the *comedia* in general, and of Calderón in particular, whom they considered as Spain's preeminent dramatist. The erroneous idea about the superficiality of the *comedia* as a reflection of the times and nothing more, must give way to a newer concept based on a serious study of one of Spain's major contributions to world literature.

IV *Understanding the* Comedia

Professor Reichenberger believes that every student of the *comedia* who wishes to understand the genre, must first understand the culture of the period.[3] Seventeenth century Spanish society was a continuation of the Middle Ages, and consisted of a hierarchy ranging from the lowly peasant to the king. Each person in this society had definite duties to perform and nobody from a lower rank could move easily to a higher one.

The *comedia* reflects this society and its ideology. In the *comedia,* therefore, there is only one protagonist—the Spanish people. The *comedia,* Reichenberger finds, rests on the firm foundation of two predominant and recurring themes—honor and faith. Honor refers to the dignity of the individual, or his reputation in the community. The Spaniard is what he is because of a strong feeling of self-respect (or pride), coupled with a desire to be respected. Reichenberger compares honor in the *comedia* with Fate in the Greek theater. Down the centuries honor has acquired a more profound meaning filled with the metaphysical value of a ritualistic nature. The act of restoring a lost honor constitutes a duty and at times a ritual in which a propitiating victim is sacrificed to an offended deity—in this case, society. Thus the community purges and renews itself constantly.

Another aspect of the honor theme is the conventional ending of a *comedia* with a plural wedding. The point is not that it matters whether the woman marries the man she loves, but that she acquires the status of a married woman.

Faith is needed to fortify man in the enigma of his destiny on earth. It resolves all conflicts in religious plays. God is always near at hand to punish the evil doer and to reward the virtuous Christian.

Professor Reichenberger considers the *comedia* a mirror of a society whose outlook on life and death has been determined by the Church in matters of faith, and by society in matters of honor. Within this narrow framework one cannot expect much "individualizing [of] distinctive traits of character."

In an attempt to explain the survival of the Greek theater with its universal appeal, Professor Reichenberger points out that the Classical theater is essentially tragic, and depicts man alone on earth struggling with dignity against supernatural forces that are more powerful than himself. Shakespearean tragedy presents man alone in the universe as in the Greek theater, fighting against mysterious forces, on a secular plane, that are inside him.

The rigid code of honor and faith, according to Dr. Reichenberger, makes tragedy, as conceived in the Classical tradition, almost impossible in Spain. It is the outcome of the plot that determines whether or not a play can be considered a tragedy. Only when a *comedia* terminates by outraging the audience's sense of justice, can it fall into the category of tragedy. A true tragedy must dash any hope for the protagonist's happiness; it need not end in his death.

V *Interpretation of the* Comedia

Professor Wade believes that it is impossible for the modern reader to say with any degree of finality exactly what a *comedia* (or any portion of it, like a word or a line) meant for a Golden Age playwright, for a variety of reasons.[4] Professor Wade quotes from T. S. Eliot's lecture, printed by the University of Minnesota Press in 1956, and entitled *The Frontiers of Criticism,* (p. 4): "every generation must provide its own literary criticism, for . . . each generation brings to the contemplation of art its own categories of appreciation, makes its own demands upon art, and has its own uses for art."

Eliot continues that the meaning of a play is never exhausted by any one explication or interpretation since it will mean different things to different sensitive readers. Moreover, the unsuspecting reader of a play always runs the risk of assuming that his interpretation "is necessarily an account of what the author was consciously or unconsciously trying to do."

Professor Wade sustains Eliot's thesis and argues that even our top-flight experts who have immersed themselves in Golden Age research may only provide us with a "pale approximation of the total meaning of a *comedia.*" Since the meaning of words is derived from their context, which means the total environment in which each word became a symbol of a particular situation, Professor Wade concludes that "it will even be impossible for us to say with finality just what a word, a phrase, or an entire play meant for Lope or for Tirso insofar as this word, phrase or play sums up a concept or a battery of concepts to explain any substantial part of the totality of Spain's Golden Age."

Professor Wade sees a future trend developing in *comedia* criticism which approaches the plays as dramatic poems in which the meaning of the play is derived from a study of its imagery. One of the most recent examples is Professor Bruce W. Wardropper's study "Poetry and Drama in Calderón's *El médico de su honra*." [5]

Another point of view in regard to understanding the *comedia* has been set forth by Professor A. A. Parker in an illuminating article in which he explains five basic principles designed to increase the reader's understanding of the *comedia*.[6] These principles that determine plot construction are, in general, applicable to the plays of most Golden Age playwrights since they all follow a continuing tradition. Professor Parker sums up his five principles as follows:

1. The primacy of action over character depiction.
2. The primacy of theme over action.
3. Dramatic unity is found more in the theme than in the action.
4. The subordination of the theme to a moral purpose through the principle of poetic justice, which is not exemplified only by the death of the wrongdoer.
5. The elucidation of the moral purpose by means of dramatic causality.

VI *Analyzing the* Comedia

What I am about to propose is not a new or revolutionary method of *comedia* analysis. It consists basically of a close reading, line by line, and sometimes word by word, in an attempt to ascertain the intrinsic meaning of the play and thus to relate form to meaning. The method also comprises quotations integrated with the critical analysis. One should proceed on the assumption that an author has an idea or a problem which he wishes to dramatize. He understands human psychology both by intuition and by common sense; he knows human behavior from observation and experience; in other words, he has all the human elements at his finger tips. If he were to stop here, however, he would be no more than an observer of facts. He must now bring his artistic genius into play.

The method of analysis may be divided into the following categories: diction, characters, theme, plot and techniques. It should not be assumed that this is necessarily the exact order of analysis. At any given moment the method of analysis may be dealing with all of these stages at once. I shall begin with a discussion of language.

Diction. The basic expressive and communicative unit of the play is its diction. The problem of diction is all-important in the creation of drama, since the author must select the right word in every instance. The dramatist has arranged his diction into meaningful patterns in the form of dialogue. One of our first tasks is to examine the cluster of images found in the dialogue. Sometimes a dramatist reinforces his meaning and ideas through the use of redundance and image cluster. At the same time that the author makes a comparison, he may also draw a contrast which has the paradoxical effect of underlining differences and similarities, and also of heightening the emotional impact. Because of the economy of time in drama, words cannot be wasted. The writer must wring every possible nuance of meaning from them.

Closely linked to diction is symbolism. How is symbolism (if any) used in the play and what is its relation to the over-all meaning? Several types of symbolism can be distinguished. First, there is the linguistic. This type need not detain us for long, since its tie-up with language and diction is obvious. The prison in *Life is a Dream* has not only its literal meaning, but in addition a figurative one: it is a womb symbol that represents the re-birth of Segismundo from a prisoner of his emotions to a man of reason.

The second type is called stage symbolism. By it is meant the physical or material things seen on the stage or referred to by the actors and having an integral bearing on the meaning of the play. In *Life is a Dream,* the sword which Rosaura carries not only identifies her with Clotaldo, who recognizes it as his own and Rosaura as his offspring, but it also represents the justice she is seeking in her attempt to clear her honor.

The third type is mythic symbolism. The area covered by this type is shared by religion, folklore, anthropology, sociology, psychoanalysis and the fine arts. Mythic symbolism, like poetry, is a kind of truth, or equivalent of truth, not a rival of historical or scientific truth, but rather a supplement. It operates through the archetypal or universal and expresses timeless ideals or truths. In *Life is a Dream,* Segismundo is not only a character of flesh and blood but, as Menéndez Pelayo has pointed out, he is a symbol of all mankind in its struggle between reason and the emotions.

Characters. As we study language, imagery and symbols, we begin to acquire an insight into the characters. Their personality may be revealed through their dialogue or through any commentary on the part of any other character. Golden Age dramatists recognized that nothing reveals personality as well as the actions and reactions of the individual himself. What a character says, what others say about him, what he does and how he reacts to others and to situations may reveal several aspects of the same man. If a change occurs in the character throughout the play, we ask ourselves the nature of the change and when and where it begins to appear. Does the character respond differently at various points in the play to a similar situation? If so, why? What does his new response disclose?

As the various characters begin to define themselves in terms of the stage action and dialogue, the principal dramatic ideas begin to take shape. We try to explain the precise relationship each character bears to the central idea of the play. How does his presence contribute to the development and modification of the action? This leads us to an analysis of the plot in its several aspects and the role each character plays in the unfolding of the *comedia.*

Plot. The plot structure is carefully studied and analyzed with a view toward ascertaining how the various episodes and incidents hang together. Does the arrangement of the scenes contribute most effectively to the over-all development of the action and do they lead logically to the climax and resolution? Is the action prepared for in advance, or is the development left to chance? Is there good timing? Does the minor action blend artistically with the main action to form one coherent harmonious entity? If there is a sub-plot, what is its function? Does it reinforce the main action by illumination or reflection?

Three important factors to be considered in plot design are: a) selection of incidents, b) arrangement and c) suspense. Since there must be economy of time and space in drama we examine the incidents to see if they have been selected to concentrate on the essentials of the main action. We want to know if there is a climactic arrangement of episodes within each act and within the play as a whole. Does one episode evolve with naturalness from the previous one? Do all the episodes advance the plot, or are there seemingly extraneous ones? Do they serve any other purpose?

The incidents must not only have interest in themselves, but they must also be arranged in such a manner that they arouse the audience's curiosity and should not prematurely reveal the denouement. This factor is called suspense. In some plays the conclusion may be intuited by the audience before the play ends, but the spectator is curious to see how the characters work out their destiny. Furthermore, there is always a certain amount of uncertainty concerning the resolution and this tantalizing doubt is usually sufficient to hold the audience's attention and interest.

Golden Age dramatists frequently develop sub-plots, parallel plots and side plots in order to enhance the reader's understanding and appreciation of the main plot. Secondary plots are seldom, if ever, mere appendages of the main plot; rather they are welded to it in such a way that their excision would all but destroy the essential unity and beauty which the author intended to convey. We have found that very frequently the secondary or back action rests on a sociological base and the main or fore action on a psychological one. This is an over-simplification, for the two actions are interdependent and interrelated, to the point where it is often difficult to separate them and often parts of the psychological and sociological are to be found in both actions, and are associated many times with a moral question.

Frequently scenes are arranged in units of one or more scenes. This unit is called a block. It is considered as a separate dramatic unity only for purposes of analysis because all the scenes center around certain characters, usually in a given place. The block of scenes usually sets forth or further develops one dramatic idea, one action mass, and attempts to achieve one unity of impression. At times it may contain the scant beginnings of the sub-plot. The next block of scenes may involve an entirely new grouping of characters and develop a new motif. One should try to discover the relationship between this new block and the preceding one, what it adds, and what it modifies. In other words, one should study each scene and block of scenes as an integral part of an evolving whole and discern what is being presented, why it is being presented at that point, and how it is executed dramatically.

Techniques. Lope de Vega, in his *Arte nuevo de hacer comedias en este tiempo* (*The New Art of Playwriting in Our Time*), specified that Act One should be devoted to exposition, Act Two to development and Act Three to denouement. In practice this did not work out exactly as Lope had prescribed. Exposition could and did appear anywhere in the *comedia* where it was needed to provide information. How is exposition handled? The necessary information an audience needs to know may be given in a conversation between secondary characters or servants at the opening, or in a long speech by any character. The inner state of a character is often described in the long speeches, asides or soliloquies. Although dialogue and monologue are the principal ways of providing exposition, they are not the only ones.

CHAPTER 3

The Spanish Theater of the Golden Age

FOR over three hundred years, i.e., from the twelfth century until the fifteenth, the Spanish theater is shrouded in the mists of uncertainty. We know from *The Seven Books of the Law* (*Las Siete Partidas*) of Alfonso el Sabio that members of the clergy were permitted to act in religious plays but were forbidden to participate in satirical plays. In the late fifteenth century Juan del Encina was writing *Eclogues* (*Eglogas*) which were performed in the castles and palaces of the nobles. About the middle of the sixteenth century comedies and farces were given in the public squares. Toward the year 1572, the Brotherhood of the Sacred Passion, a group of charitable citizens of Madrid, had as their main purpose to provide funds for the city's hospitals.[1] The Brotherhood obtained the monopoly of providing a place to stage dramatic performances and applied the box office receipts to the commendable aim of raising money for the hospitals. In 1574 the Brotherhood of the Solitude of Our Lady opposed the monopoly. But an amicable settlement was arranged whereby both contributed to the expenses of the hospitals. In 1579 the two Brotherhoods bought a house in the street called de la Cruz which they proceeded to convert into a theater. In 1582 they acquired property on Príncipe Street where they opened another theater. These two theaters continued without a rival until the opening of the Caños de Peral theater in the early seventeenth century.

The early theaters of Madrid were known as *corrales,* originally the back yards of houses before they were converted into places of amusement.[2] At one end was the stage; the audience witnessed the performance by standing in the courtyard known as the patio. There was no roof to protect the audience and actors from the hot sun or a sudden downpour of rain. If the weather became inclement, the performance was terminated or suspended temporarily until conditions permitted its resumption.

Performances were scheduled for Sundays and holidays at three o'clock in summer and two in winter. Later, as the theater became more popular, additional performances were given on Tuesdays and Thursdays. All representations were suspended during Lent and periods of mourning or pestilence.

The performance began with a prologue (*loa*) that sometimes, but not always, was related to the play which followed. Two interludes (*entremeses*), usually farcical in nature, were performed between the acts. The entire performance concluded with a jig, or perhaps a short farce called a *sainete*.

Sometimes dances were given between acts or during the play itself. A great variety of dances were in vogue during the seventeenth century: the *Zarabanda, Chacona, Seguidilla* and the *Gallarda,* to name but a few. Some of the dances were a bit risqué and it frequently became necessary for the authorities to halt them.

The theaters themselves at first were rather crude and had few facilities for the comfort of the audience and actors. As time went by, benches were set up near the stage and an awning protected the spectators from the sun. The windows of the houses which surrounded the patio served as box seats for those who could afford them, and we may be sure that members of the aristocracy had their box seats year after year. Members of the Town Council and the clergy too had private boxes and from this vantage point were able to view a performance without having to rub elbows with the motley throng of standees that crowded the patio.

In the rear of the theater was a special balcony reserved for women and called the "stewpan" (*cazuela*). Women who wished to maintain their good reputation concealed their identity behind a mask. A policeman (*alguacil*) was posted at the entrance to the women's gallery to prevent men from entering.

The stage itself, like the Elizabethan, was almost devoid of scenery. The audience knew the setting from the dialogue. Curtains (*paños*), if necessary, were hung at the sides of the stage and this was indicated in the stage directions. A curtain at the back of the stage could be opened to simulate an interior scene.

Above it, also in the background, was a balcony that could represent a mountain, a town, the upper window of a house, the walls of a town, etc. The dressing rooms for the actors were located in a space set apart near the stage and separated from the audience by a curtain. It was also used by the musicians who played for the musical numbers.

Double admission was exacted from theatergoers at this time. First, the manager collected his fee at the entrance. Just inside the door a cleric demanded another contribution which was destined for the hospitals. In those days it was deemed a distinction to crash the gate and enter without paying the price of admission. Juan de Zabaleta in his book, *The Afternoon of a Feast Day* (*Día de fiesta por la tarde*), Madrid, 1692, relates the practice: "the first thing one does is to try to enter without paying. The first misfortune of players is to work a lot and to have only a few persons pay. Everybody wishes to enjoy the privilege of free admission in order that others may see that they are worthy of it. This they desire with such intense eagerness that they will fight to obtain it, and by fighting they achieve their objective. Rarely does a man who has once quarreled to avoid paying ever pay at any subsequent time." Then as now ticket speculators scalped the public when a popular play or well known actor or actress was to appear on the boards.

Refreshments like fruit, candy and sweetened drinks were sold between acts.

The audience was often highly critical, noisy and on occasion disorderly. The rabble, which assembled in the patio to view a performance from a standing position, was especially feared by both actors and dramatists. It came provided with rattles, fresh (or perhaps spoiled) fruit and vegetables and could whistle, heckle and bombard the actors on the stage. Lope, who earlier realized that the success or failure of a play depended on this formidable segment of the audience, catered to it and addressed it often as "illustrious senate," while on other less risky occasions he scornfully referred to it as the "mob."

During the zenith of the Spanish *comedia* between 1610 and 1650, there were more than a dozen theatrical companies in Spain. They had to be licensed by the King and were subject to perform at the royal command. They acted not only in Madrid but in other cities like Valencia, Seville and Valladolid. Each company numbered between fourteen to twenty persons besides the director. Often actors had to play two or three roles since the cast of many *comedias* at times exceeded the number of players in a company. At first women were not permitted on the boards and female parts were played by boys.

The actors were recruited from the lower classes of society. They led less than virtuous lives and were fond of gambling. They were hired on a contractual basis for a period of one or two years. Salaries varied and depended on the histrionic talent of the performer and his drawing power with the public.

During the reign of Philip IV (1621–1665), plays were performed not only in the theaters but also in the old palace (*Alcázar*) before royalty. But this gloomy and austere edifice was not suited for joyous festivals and tended to depress the spirit of the monarch. Around the year 1629, the King's Prime Minister, the Count-Duke of Olivares, conceived the idea of a new palace and new grounds with formal gardens. This new palace, called the Buen Retiro, was opened in 1634, a date that marks the rise of the court theater. Calderón composed an *auto sacramental* (a one-act religious piece dealing with the Eucharist), *The New Palace of the Retiro* (*El nuevo palacio del Retiro*), performed in the spring of that year. It mentions various things of the period like the equestrian statue of Philip, a statue of Charles V, the gardens, fountains with statue of Narcissus, pools, aviary, etc.

A special room called the *Coliseo del Buen Retiro* was set aside for performances of plays. On special occasions performances were held at night outdoors in the gardens and on the lagoons. On the 23rd of June, 1635 Calderón's *Love, the Greatest Enchanter* (*El mayor encanto, amor*) was performed on an isle in the lagoon of the gardens of the Buen Retiro.[3] The King and his party were viewing the show from gondolas when a sudden windstorm extinguished the more than three thousand lights and overturned some of the boats. The play was halted and given a few days later. The performance lasted six hours, and ended at one in the morning. The decorations were executed by Cosme Lotti who had been brought from Italy in 1626 to design the fountains and gardens.

The Beast, The Thunderbolt and The Stone (*La fiera, el rayo y la piedra*) was performed in 1652 on a grandiose scale in celebration of Queen Mariana's birthday. The Italian artist Vaggio designed the decorations and scenic effects. The performance was given at night and had to be illuminated with many lights. The scenery was complicated and the numerous scene changes ran the performance to seven hours. The royal family and the court attended the premiere while the general public was admitted on succeeding days. Later the play enjoyed a run of thirty-seven days and played to capacity audiences. The admittance of the general public to attend plays in the palace attests to the intimacy between people and monarch and is proof of the deep roots of the monarchy in the national consciousness.

From the text of *The Three Greatest Prodigies* (*Los tres mayores prodigios*), we know that three different companies performed the work on three different stages. About seventy of Calderón's plays were staged at the court, many of them before royalty.

Enormous sums of money were spent on these lavish court productions, replete with music, singing and dancing. Elaborate stage sets and effects to produce the many spectaculars necessitated the importation of Italian artists who also created other peripheral attractions like statuary and fountains.

After 1651, the year in which Calderón became a priest, the majority of his plays were mythological in theme and were almost always accompanied by music. This type of play was best suited to his flights of poetic fancy, and at the same time provided greater freedom of expression for the galaxy of artists, engineers and musicians. These plays were truly court luxuries much in the manner of the operas of Quinault and Lulli, the most admired poet and composer team of the French capital. The brilliancy of these spectacles with their intricate stage machinery, elaborate scenery and gorgeous costumes made the Spanish court one of the most dazzling of all Europe.

CHAPTER 4

Facets of Calderón's Dramatic and Poetic Art

CALDERON'S dramatic art belongs to the period known as the high baroque; it is characterized by balance and contrast in regard to imagery, linguistic style, plot structure and character portrayal. His imagery is rich in its profusion and at times profound in the range of meaning it suggests. It was greatly influenced by the poetic fads of the day—the Gongorism and conceptism discussed in Chapter 1.

I *Imagery*

Calderón's poetic images are largely visual. They are drawn from the cosmos, mythology, the court, nature, light and the animal world. From nature the poet borrows images of landscapes—wild, barren, rugged—to underline the unchecked passions of man. He depicts cataclysmic manifestations of nature on the rampage to portend a fatal event. From astronomy Calderón takes images to describe the beauty of woman and the majesty of kingship. He employs images of light to represent reason, human life, love and truth. From mythology he selects figures, characters and fabled animals to express universal truths, emotional imbalance and the hybrid nature of man. From the animal kingdom he chooses the horse to convey the meanings of fate and pride, and the eagle to connote the Hapsburg lineage of royalty. By a combination of images involving animals and nature he is able to epitomize the idea of chaos in the emotional, mental, moral and political state of man. To show more vividly man's emotional disturbance, the dramatist resorts to the unusual: hybrid animals, monsters, desolate or densely covered landscapes and often extraordinary displays of nature such as eclipses and the eruptions of volcanos.

The concept of the four elements of fire, air, earth and water which played so basic a role in the classical understanding of the universe had been integrated into the scholastic system. The notion held by the ancients that the harmony of the four elements separated order from chaos reached the status of a belief. Calderón found the idea useful to explain natural law. He also dramatized the conflict of the elements to show man's imperfection and his dependence upon the equilibrium of the elements for his salvation. To express motion or violent action, Calderón may refer to any one of the four elements in terms of the others. Thus to underscore the speed of a ship he calls it a "bird of the sea," or a "horse of the sea." [1]

II *Linguistic Style*

Calderón's linguistic style is highly formalized and is punctuated by many rhetorical flourishes and stylized devices which follow the classical poetic tradition.

Simile and Metaphor. Simile and metaphor are high on his list. To stress the speed of a horse Calderón likens it to the hippogriff, the fabled animal whose wings are indicative of its ability to hurl itself through space at a rapid rate. Usually the dramatist is not content to employ one comparison at a time; he is fond of the repetition and accumulation of comparisons.

Play on Words. A play on words (*equívoco*) was thought by the eighteenth-century critics to be an example of bad taste, but modern critics now consider such an embellishment as an admired feature of baroque expression. A special kind of ingenious play on words designated as a paronomasia involves vocables that sound almost alike but have different meanings:

(¡Que un *hombre* con tanta *hambre!*)
To think that a man with so much hunger!
(*Life is a Dream*)

Calderón was also fond of playing with names; one recalls an untranslatable play on words from *The Wonder-Working Magician* (*El mágico prodigioso*):

(. . . llega Livia,
al *na*, y sé, Livia, *liviana.*)

The chiaroscuro. Another aspect of Calderón's baroque style is the *chiaroscuro* or light and shadow effect:

Is not that dim light some expiring breath, some pale star which, in tremulous flickerings, in pulsating ardors and throbbing rays, makes more obscure the dark room with doubtful light?

(*Life is a Dream*)

¿No es breve luz aquella
caduca exhalación, pálida estrella,
que en trémulos desmayos,
pulsando ardores y latiendo rayos,
hace más tenebrosa
la oscura habitación con luz dudosa?)
(*La vida es sueño*)

Oxymoron. An oxymoron is a figure of speech in which an adjective implies the contrary of the noun that it modifies. Calderón was fond of violent contrasts to heighten the impact upon his reader:

being a living skeleton,
being an animated corpse.
(*Life is a Dream*)

(siendo un esqueleto vivo,
siendo un animado muerto.)
(*La vida es sueño.*)

Catachresis. A catachresis is a rhetorical device and figure of speech in which a word is applied to an object outside the word's usual range of meaning. Thus the combination of terms often turns out to be an overstrained metaphor bordering on distortion. For example, a male character, greeting a female relative in formal court-terms, refers to the salvo of trumpets and the chattering of birds in a kind of cross reference:

some, feathered trumpets,
others, birds of metal.
(*Life is a Dream*)

(¡unos, clarines de pluma,
y otras, aves de metal!)
(*La vida es sueño*)

Chiasmus. Defined as a balancing of the members of the ends against those of the middle, the chiasmus is a common stylistic feature of Calderón's art. In *Life is a Dream,* the protagonist refers to himself as follows:

I am a man among beasts,
and a beast among men.
(soy un hombre de las fieras
y una fiera de los hombres.)

Parody. Parody is often found in Calderón's art. When a male character in *Life is a Dream* first meets one of the female characters, he parodies the words, *"bien"* (good) and *"parabién"* (good wishes or congratulations):

Although it is good to receive your good wishes for the good which I have received, the only good that I can admit is having seen you today; and so I am grateful to you for the good wishes, a good which I really don't deserve.

(Aunque el parabién es bien
darme el bien que conquisto,
de sólo haberos hoy visto
os admito el parabién;
y así, del llegarme a ver
con el bien que no merezco,
el parabién agradezco.)

Dialectics and Casuistry. Dialectics and casuistry are hallmarks of Calderón's art. The syllogism is one of the most common forms of reasoning he employs, and closely allied to it is reasoning by analogy and from example. Sometimes the debate takes the form of a pseudo-disputation by the use of rhetorical questions. To give even greater emphasis to dialectics, Calderón propels a dramatic conflict by means of the antithesis of two words or ideas. Concatenation or accumulation of arguments is another favorite device.

Dialectics and casuistry are used for persuasion in matters religious, philosophical, moral, ethical and erotic. They reveal the mental anguish of a character, and justify his course of conduct. Sometimes they create comic effect and at other times they heighten the lyrical impression. They are characterized by such features as the stylization of formulae, stereotyped terminology, and antithesis and parallel structure in the pro and con of the debate.

At first glance Calderón's *racionalismo* (rationalism) seems to possess the quality of a never-ending search for new truth, but a closer scrutiny reveals that there is always a truth in his mind which is fixed and complete for all eternity. The dialectical method is in no way investigatory; it is an Aristotelian device which in Calderón's theater draws the consequences from truths already acknowledged through the teachings of the Church, rather than through seeking new truths. The convolutions of controlled arguments do no more than simulate the search for truth; their real value lies in the dramatic conflict they depict and the emotional impact they produce on the audience and reader.

Accumulation of ideas. This is little more than rhetorical embellishment, designed for greater emotional impact through parallel use of certain parts of speech. In the following example, Calderón masses nouns, verbs and possessive adjectives:

mi seguridad te pido,
mis temores desvanezco,
mis quietudes facilito,
mis deseos aseguro,
mis contentos solicito,
mis recelos acobardo,
mis esperanzas animo.
(*Jealousy, the Greatest Monster*)

III *Plot Structure*

Calderón develops the action of a play by means of a single or a double plot. A single action moves forward as a linear progression implemented by parallels and contrasts in the manipulation of theme, characters and imagery. Where there is a double plot, the two actions alternate and are progressively knotted until they fuse. The fusion may take place in Act Two or Act Three. The plots are sometimes linked thematically as in *Absalom's Hair* (*Los cabellos de Absalón*), where the rape of Tamar (lust of the flesh) is associated with the rape of the state (lust for power).

The opening scene of a play plunges the reader or spectator *in medias res* to capture immediate audience interest. Sometimes a young lady may stumble or pretend to stumble in order to win a gentleman's attention. Sometimes a character has a problem in dire need of a solution. Background information of what happened before the play opened is given in a flashback (*relación*). The flashback may occur anywhere to provide the audience with the information it needs in order to understand the play, but it is usually found early in Act One. It is almost always introduced by some form of the verb *escuchar* (to listen) or *oír* (to hear).

Regardless of whether or not the plot is single or double, it is developed piecemeal, segment by segment, somewhat as a rosebud unfolds gradually into a beautiful flower. The author relates the characters to each other and ultimately effects the confrontation of protagonist and antagonist. The intensity of the action rises within each act to a crisis; acts usually end on a climactic note. In the last act, crisis precipitates the major climax and the resolution takes place immediately, or in what little action, denoted as the falling action, is left. At the points of climax and resolution, all of the important characters are on the stage and all the needed explanations are given for complete audience comprehension.

Conflict is generally depicted on at least two levels: as an exterior clash between two opposing forces (antagonist versus protagonist) and as a disruption experienced within the mind of one or more of the leading characters. The internal struggle brought about by forces outside or inside a character is often the major reality that gives a play its significance. A common device to create audience suspense is the interruption of a character who is about to reveal important information.

IV *Characterization*

Ever since Aristotle declared that character should be subordinate to action there has been confusion in the minds of critics and theorists of drama. In the case of Calderón, the Aristotelian generalization may be true for his mediocre plays. But in his masterworks character determines the plot, since the situations that will arise develop from character and spring logically from it. Indeed, Calderón has provided a number of excellent character portrayals. One thinks, for example, of Segismundo in *Life is a Dream* (*La vida es sueño*), of old Pedro Crespo in *The Mayor of Zalamea* (*El alcalde de Zalamea*), of Eusebio in *The Devotion to the Cross* (*La devoción de la cruz*), or of Semíramis in *Daughter of the Air* (*La hija del aire*). In addition, he has left some excellent portraits of minor characters, in such low-life figures as La Chispa and Rebolledo in *The Mayor of Zalamea.* Both major and minor characters in his outstanding plays are persons of flesh and blood endowed with all the major emotions of the seventeenth-century Spaniard. Sometimes, however, Calderón presents his best creations, like Segismundo, larger than life, so to speak, so that the prince becomes a symbol of mankind. Semíramis, like Lady Macbeth, may be viewed as a symbol of evil. Of Calderón's female characters, however, very few are depicted in any great detail. The mother is almost entirely absent from his plays—as in all Golden Age *comedias*—unless she has some unusually important dramatic function. One outstanding mother, though thoroughly denigrated in the play, is the Empress Semíramis.

The characters are usually well orchestrated; that is, they are not all alike. One or more characters may be more sharply defined than the rest whose figures are enveloped in a misty haze. This technique is sometimes called the "law of subordination."

Some characters in the Calderonian repertory remain the same throughout the play; that is, they are unbending in their attitude and point of view. The Captain in *The Mayor of Zalamea* will never change for the better, and is in opposition to the ideals of Pedro Crespo as well as to the social conventions of the period. The unbending quality of his attitude provides the intensifying conflict of the play. Many of the characters of Calderón's drama suffer from an excessive pride which is left unchecked and brings about their downfall. As for Segismundo of *Life is a Dream,* he is in conflict with all those he meets, although during the course of the drama, his character evinces a change and by the final curtain he has undergone a basic transformation. Cipriano in *The Wonder-Working Magician* (*El mágico prodigioso*) likewise changes, moving from evil to good.

Most plays contain a number of stock characters. The *gracioso* or clown is usually a servant. He is garrulous and is addicted to eating and drinking. He was considered so important for comic relief by the writers of the Golden Age *comedia* that he was included even in religious and serious plays. Servants were often used as confidants of their masters to eavesdrop on important conversations and relay messages to advance the action. The father, esquire or some older person served as the guardian of the heroine. Sometimes it was the girl's brother who was assigned the custody of her honor.

Professor Oppenheimer sees Calderonian characters in revolt against the stringent social patterns in their attempt to achieve self-realization.[2] Under the influence of Humanism they act out of emotional needs and desires in such a way as to break normal behavior patterns and seem out of step with the logical development of the plot. Oppenheimer concludes that the characters ultimately realize their human limitations and resolve their difficulties in an "illusory harmonious synthesis of discordant elements: this is Baroque."

V *Thematic Cluster*

One of the reasons why there have been so many interpretations of any one of Calderón's plays is that the dramatist may deal with a variety of themes all related in varying degrees to the main theme of the work. In the welter of thematic confusion, the reader may have difficulty in determining which is the principal theme and which are the subordinate ones. In the dramas on jealousy, for example, other themes related to it such as love, hate, envy, infidelity, truth and death also play important roles. The effect of multiple themes is to endow the play with a greater degree of reality and naturalness, thus mirroring life itself. Moreover, the multiplicity of themes produces the bewilderment, doubt and confusion found in life which Calderón dramatizes throughout his repertory.

VI *Techniques*

The Soliloquy. The soliloquy is the vehicle par excellence to portray the changing manifestations of a character's mental struggle often expressed through finespun reasoning. A pattern may be established whereby an individual reviews his predicament and weighs the consequences of alternative paths of action before reaching a decision. In many cases the soliloquy serves to convey a plausible explanation of an action, or of an attitude of which the real, though often unconscious, motive is of such a nature that one would consciously disavow it. Sometimes Calderón employs argumentation in the form of the soliloquy as a substitute for action. That is, the soliloquy may reveal character just as action may.

The Flashback (*relación*). Closely akin to the soliloquy is the long-winded speech designed to impart information to the audience regarding events which took place prior to the opening of the play. This type of exposition usually occurs near the beginning of the first act. At times there may be exposition toward the middle or end of the third act to clear up doubts and complete the recounting of a previously interrupted narration. A variation is the pause in the action so that a character may bring his colleagues up to date on what has happened. The pause also gives the audience (or reader) time to review the situation before another sequence of events is unfolded. The tendency of all this protracted speech is to delay the culmination of the action; this interruption in the flow of events helps to increase the suspense, but it may result in producing boredom in the modern reader.

Meters. All of Calderón's plays, like those of his contemporaries, were written in verse.[3] He follows Lope de Vega generally in regard to the use of meters: *romance* and *redondilla* for dialogue, narration and exposition; *silva* and *décima* for serious actions often involving characters of the higher echelons of society; *silva* for dialogue of a more lyric tone; *soneto* for soliloquy; *décima* or *octava* for special effects and *quintilla* for narration in palace scenes.

Often Calderón changes a meter within a scene to indicate a change in mood. The same meter may spill over into another scene, or continue for several scenes. The same spill-over technique in the use of meters may occur in the same act even when there are primary and secondary actions.

Dialogue. Even though the dialogue is cast in verse, it does not seem unnatural. In a play like *The Mayor of Zalamea* where the action has a strong ring of realism, the conversation is likewise realistic, from the chatter of the picaresque characters to the arguments between the mayor and the gouty old general. To stress haste or emotional upset, Calderón favors sticomythic (or dove-tailed) dialogue in which one character in staccato-like fashion completes in a few words what another has started to say.

Anecdotal Material. Occasionally Calderón relies on anecdotal material to emphasize a point. In *Life is a Dream,* on finding that Segismundo is so wretched and a fellow companion in misery, Rosaura relates briefly an anecdote the point of which is applicable to her own situation. It is the story of a man who was so poor that he felt sorry for himself until he found another eating what he threw away.

Asides. An aside is a device used to reveal the true feelings of a character, usually surprise or fear. Editors are likely to set it apart from the rest of the text by enclosing it in parentheses. The word "*aparte*" (aside) is sometimes indicated outside the lines or part-lines of the text that are to be read as an aside. When almost an entire speech is interrupted by asides in every line, the effect is to increase the suspense and sharpen the emotional intensity of the passage.

Recapitulation. Recapitulation is a summary of the various words, usually nouns, employed as parts of a comparison. The recapitulation may summarize the words in an inverse order or in the same order in which they were first presented. In *Life is a Dream,* the protagonist Segismundo cannot understand why he has been deprived of his freedom. He compares himself to a bird, a beast, a fish and a stream, all of which have no soul but more freedom. Then he sums up the comparison in reverse order, asking what law can deny to men the cherished privilege God has given to a stream, a fish, a beast and a bird.

VII *Fusion of the Arts*

A fusion of music, painting and scenic effects permeates Calderón's lavish court spectacle, *Love the Greatest Enchanter* (*El mayor encanto, amor*), performed in 1635 on three stages by three different companies of players in the formal gardens of the Buen Retiro palace.

Baroque sensibility assimilated the sphere of the natural world and man's world of the arts. In a tract on painting written in 1677, Calderón admitted he had always felt a natural inclination toward painting which he defined as an imitation of God's handiwork and emulation of nature.[4] He believed that all the arts had their origin in God and were designed to serve the Creator's purposes.

That Calderón borrowed metaphors and conceits from painting can be seen in his descriptions of court ceremonies, festivities and the formal gardens. One can find examples in such plays as *The House with Two Doors* (*Casa con dos puertas*), (to be discussed in Chapter 5); *The Sash and the Flower* (*La banda y la flor*), and *Beware of Smooth Water* (*Guárdate del agua mansa*).

Calderón's art is a synthesis of many facets of his learning: mythology, rhetoric, logic, philosophy, theology and law, all neatly integrated into the various plays of his repertory.

E. R. Curtius has given us a succinct and adequate evaluation of Calderón's style:

"The mannered ornamental style of a Calderón was understood and enjoyed by the Madrid public, always eager for a good show. His recondite images and comparisons were borne on the stream of a ringing rhetoric which delighted the ears even of the common man. To the *conceptos,* with their plays on words and ideas, the common man was receptive too. The imagery of writing and the book was for the most part, as we have seen, a private domain for educated, if not for erudite, circles. Calderón makes it popular once again; at the same time he represents its final apogee in Western poetry." [5]

CHAPTER 5

The Cloak-and-Sword Plays

THE Cloak-and-Sword plays are thus called because of the cloak and sword worn by the gentlemen of the era. This type of play reached its zenith with Calderón. Its purpose was mostly to amuse. It contained the zestful ingredients of a romantic love universal in its appeal: boy meets girl (sometimes girl pursues boy). All kinds of obstacles arise to thwart an immediate marriage, especially a vigilant father, brother or other relative. The audience is kept on edge by the rapidity of the action, the excitement of the chase and the various intrigues, duels, deceits, misunderstandings, cross-purposes, miraculous escapes and the moral issues involved. There is charm in the naturalness of the dialogue, the brilliant repartee and the lyric verses.

The source of most plays of this type is in Latin comedy, in the inventiveness of the author, or in the works of immediate predecessors. The characters are usually the same and become almost stereotyped: two or three suitors, and their corresponding ladies, a father or squire and servants, the confidants of their masters. Some representative plays are: *The House with Two Doors* (*Casa con dos puertas mala es de guardar*), *The Phantom Lady* (*La dama duende*), *The False Astrologer* (*El astrólogo fingido*), *Mornings in April and May* (*Mañanas de abril y mayo*), *The Dancing Teacher* (*El maestro de danzar*) and *The Hidden Man and The Veiled Lady* (*El escondido y la tapada*). Not unlike the Cloak-and-Sword play is the Palace play in which the characters are of the upper nobility. Examples are *Woman, Weep and Conquer* (*Mujer, llora y vencerás*), and *The Name's Fortune and Misfortune* (*Dicha y desdicha del nombre*). We shall now consider one of the best of the Cloak-and-Sword type, *The House with Two Doors* (*Casa con dos puertas*).

I *The House with Two Doors* (*Casa con dos puertas mala es de guardar*)

The House with Two Doors is a brilliant *tour de force* of love intrigue enacted against the backdrop of the seventeenth-century Spanish capital and its social whirl. A courtly ambient pervades the work in its multiple aspects: imagery, *milieu,* the ingenious plot structure and the behavior of its amorous suitors and ladies, who are portrayed in as stylized a fashion as the formal gardens of the Aranjuez palace where the play was probably first performed for the amusement of Queen Isabel de Borbón in 1629.[1]

Plot Summary—Lisardo, a young gentleman from Madrid, has just returned from the wars in Flanders and is seeking preferment at court. The King is at present at the palace in Aranjuez, not far from Ocaña where Lisardo is staying at the home of a friend of his college days, Félix. Because Félix, the typically tyrannical brother of the Golden Age *comedia,* fears for the good name of his sister, Marcela, if people should learn that she is permitted to see Lisardo, he orders her to keep out of sight. But the veiled Marcela has seen the handsome stranger and is determined to meet him. In the first scene of the play, she talks with him in the street not far from her home; they had met on six successive mornings at a convent near Ocaña. Lisardo is greatly smitten, although he has not learned her name nor seen her face. This morning, however, she lifts her veil and he is even more taken with love. She asks him not to follow her, promising to name herself soon and to let him come to her home.

Taking leave of Marcela, Lisardo goes on to Félix's house. There, Félix tells him of his amorous woes: having loved Laura once, he has now forsaken her for Nise. But Laura, learning of the affair, has told Nise of Félix's love for her, and Nise is now cool toward him. As Félix tells Lisardo his story, Marcela listens, concealed by a door. Lisardo starts to tell Félix of the beautiful girl he has recently been seeing. Fortunately for Marcela, who might have been identified by Lisardo's description, his story is interrupted by the arrival of Celia, Laura's maid. Laura wants Félix to come and see her, although she has Celia pretend that the interview has been arranged by the maid without the knowledge of her mistress.

In his talk with Laura, Félix, with apparent sincerity, assures her that he loves her only; he no longer cares for Nise. They are interrupted by the arrival of Fabio, Laura's father, and Félix escapes through a second street door (hence the "house with two doors" of the play's title).

Marcela induces her friend Laura to let her use her (Laura's) house as her own in which to receive Lisardo. When Lisardo arrives, his confusion over Marcela's identity is not clarified by her evasive words. When they are interrupted by Fabio's entrance, Lisardo hides in an inner room. Fabio takes Marcela to her home nearby; during his absence, Laura's plan to get Lisardo out of the house fails when Félix suddenly appears; he has come to confirm his appointment with Laura for a later hour that evening. In the meantime, Fabio returns. Seeking to avoid detection, Félix enters the room in which Lisardo is hiding in order to conceal himself there. Both men see each other but without recognition in the darkened room. Félix suspects Laura of double-dealing. He leaves (after telling Fabio that he had come for Marcela), but returns soon afterward to confront the man he had seen in the room. While Fabio and Laura are in another part of the house, Celia dismisses Lisardo. Félix accuses Laura of treachery, and she is unable to explain the truth of the situation because of her fear of betraying Marcela's interest in Lisardo.

The tempo of the action is stepped up as the four lovers become more and more enmeshed in a complex situation that involves jealousy, the persistent attempt by Marcela to keep Félix from discovering her dealings with Lisardo, Laura's effort to retain her faith in Félix's love in spite of her fear that he still loves Nise, and Lisardo's unsuccessful efforts to identify Marcela. The house with two doors is the scene of most of the action, as one or another of the characters enters and leaves. All of this to Fabio's discomfiture, as he discovers afresh the truth of the ancient Spanish proverb that a house with two doors is indeed hard to guard.

The play ends with a typically rapid dénouement: the four lovers and Fabio confront each other with initial confusion and then with a comprehension of the truth of the situation. There is mutual happiness as a "multiple marriage," so common to the

Golden Age *comedia,* is arranged, that of Lisardo and Marcela, and that of Félix and Laura.

Plot Structure and Technical Devices—The stylization of balance and contrast for which Calderón had so strong a penchant is found not only in the linguistic style and imagery but also in the arrangement of the plot. The main plot deals with Lisardo's love affair with Marcela, who has been forbidden by her brother Félix to see or converse with the guest in the house. The secondary plot centers around the love affair of Félix and Laura which is held in suspension by the latter's jealousy over Félix's former love for Nise.

There is symmetry in the friendship of the two suitors, Lisardo and Félix, and the two ladies, Marcela and Laura. Both women really want to marry their respective suitors, but are prevented from doing so by a brother and father respectively.

Since Marcela has been forbidden to speak to Lisardo, she prevails upon Laura to permit her the use of her house for a rendezvous. Since the house has two doors, it will be easy for Lisardo to visit Marcela freely. This arrangement is fraught with danger because of the possibility that Laura's father, Fabio, or her lover, Félix, may discover the strange man (Lisardo) in the house.

Comic situations arise because of the discrepancy between illusion and reality. They are accentuated by the compromising circumstances in which the characters find themselves. When Laura's father, Fabio, returns home unexpectedly, Lisardo is forced to hide in another room. A temporary solution to the dilemma is found when Fabio offers to escort Marcela home since night has fallen. During Fabio's absence Laura hopes to have Celia usher Lisardo out of the house, but at the inopportune moment Félix arrives to visit Laura, since he has seen her father leave in the company of Marcela. Just before Fabio returns, Félix hides in the same unlighted room with Lisardo, whose figure he has seen but whose identity he does not know. Félix invents the pretext that he has come for his sister. While Celia ushers Lisardo out of the house, Félix re-enters, posing as a servant. He meets Laura and upbraids her for harboring a strange man in her room.

This situation turns on the appearance-versus-reality theme brought about by misunderstandings, deceptions, veiled ladies, hidden suitors, darkness and a house with two doors. Circumstances and fate have contrived to create a "reality" of jealousy for Félix and Laura and another man. It is not a true love triangle as Lisardo, the third party, is in love with Marcela.

A parallel situation develops regarding Lisardo and Marcela. The former's mental anguish is due to his ignorance of the identity of the veiled lady he has met. She appears to be Félix's sweetheart, and if Lisardo continues courting her, he fears he will be deceiving his best friend. So in desperation he decides to pack his bags and leave.

Lisardo's gift of a traveling-suit to Calabazas, his lackey, provides the latter with the opportunity to satirize the dishonesty of tailors. On first reading, this passage may seem digressive and one may be apt to dismiss it as nothing more than an opportunity for a clever actor to display his histrionic ability by simulating two voices. But after further reflection, one may be inclined to see in it an additional intention on the part of the author, viz., that of underlining the theme of deception. Its realistic language contrasts with the conventional courtly speech of ladies and gentlemen.

The mutual distrust existing between the lovers causes Laura and Marcela to exchange houses. Laura will stay at Marcela's to ascertain if the veiled woman (Marcela) was Nise. Félix wants Marcela to spy on Laura because he suspects the latter of infidelity.

The crisis is reached when Félix is about to lose his mind over the confusion brought about by mistaken identity in the dark, and concealed identity. Explanations are in order and the characters appear one by one for the climax.

As we have seen, the play makes use of many of the stock devices inherited from the tradition of classical Roman comedy as it was known in the works of Plautus and Terence, and then continued in the Italianate comedy of intrigue and to some extent in the stylized *commedia dell'arte:* improvisations, narrowness of escapes, lies, clever excuses, eavesdropping, manipulation of the intrigue whereby characters are brought together at the right time or kept apart, disguises, mistaken identity, cross purposes, trickery, misunderstandings and surprise disclosures, all of which in total produce an effect of suspense, bewilderment and comic irony. The element of chance plays a prominent role in this type of comedy. The purpose of the intrigue is to create a farcical situation which reveals character or satirizes manners and customs of the day.

Style—The linguistic style and imagery are full of the spiral gyrations of conceptual and formal language, particularly characteristic of the seventeenth century Spanish court.

Imagery. The opening speech by Lisardo contains flowery metaphors punctuated by flattery and expressed in terms of balance and contrast. Lisardo confesses he cannot desist from following a certain lady any more than the sunflower can cease turning to the sun, the magnetic needle to the north star and the steel to the needle.

A metaphor of split imagery occurs when Félix refers to the roses, that is, the streets and the squares, left by the feet of a lady as she trod the paths of the formal gardens of the palace. The split imagery in antithetical balance is contained in the description of her dress, which is "courtly" and "rustic." The feather in her hat might be a bird of the "earth" or a flower of the "air." This interchange of the attributes of the creatures of one sphere for those of another was a commonplace, and has already been discussed in Chapter Two. Félix continues the split imagery relating how he was able to speak to her when their only witnesses were the "night" and the "garden" with their stars and flowers respectively.

In Act One Félix saw a woman reclining by a fountain in the palace gardens gazing at her beauty in the waters. She was as still as a statue and Nature seemed to say to Art: "I know how to make a statue if you know how to make a woman."

Marcela's boldness in calling to Lisardo in Act Two seemed innocent enough; it was, in Calderón's words, like the calm sea that beckoned voyagers to travel upon it. Later the storm broke and also imminent danger—a character narrating an anecdote finds it applicable to his own situation. Marcela, who has been comparing love to the sea, then applies the comparison to her own dilemma: "Thus did I judge the sea of love to be calm; but hardly did I recognize its flattery when I felt its violence."

Félix's long speech on the royal hunt at Aranjuez in Act Three is full of ornate and flowery imagery that is in harmony with the artistic tastes of the time. It reflects the court ambient in which Calderón lived and wrote.[2]

Linguistic style. An important aspect of Calderón's style occurs after Marcela rebuffs Lisardo for his boldness in addressing her without the formality of an introduction. The latter attempts to justify his conduct in a speech filled with dialectics and casuistry, arguing that he would rather be "discourteous" than "foolish." Finespun reasoning in matters of love and honor permeates most of Calderón's work. The constant reasoning or debate throughout the play lends a note of conflict albeit an artificial one.

In trying to disclaim his former love for another girl, Félix informs Laura that his love for Nise was only a "rehearsal" in which he was learning the meaning of true love. Félix then presents his case, arguing from analogy and example. He relates how a blind man, imagining what the sun would be like, recovered his sight one night, and seeing a star mistook it for the sun. Then Félix applies the anecdote to himself: "I, too, was blind and could not see the sun. I saw a star and entertained myself with it until I saw the sun itself." Laura thinks she is the star and Nise the sun, but Félix reassures her that such arguments are "self-deception," and observes that she is really suffering from "jealousy."

The cut and dried formality of the linguistic style and imagery seems highly artificial and insipid today, but it served to create the courtly atmosphere of the Madrid society in which the action took place and with which Calderón was familiar because of his association with the royal theater. Furthermore, it was appropriate to the veiled language then in vogue to express matters of the heart.

Character Delineation—The character portrayals are the weakest part of the play's fabric. The men are for the most part insipid; Félix is purposely depicted as so confused and anguished by the time the play approaches its end that his plight precipitates the beginning of the climax. The females are a little better portrayed; characteristically they are on the deceitful side in order to "get their man." Marcela is probably the best delineated of all the characters; she is a major factor in determining the flow of the action. She is forward, clever, deceitful, selfish and bold. In her love affair with Lisardo, it is Marcela who speaks first. To circumvent her brother's watchful eye on her honor, she resorts to flattery in order to gain Laura's permission to use the latter's house as a rendezvous. When her plans are thwarted, she conveniently forgets the obligation of friendship and holds to the policy of self-interest.

Her counterpart in the other love affair, Laura, is less adroitly drawn, and is somewhat of a dim reflection of Marcela. Laura is easily swayed by her friend Marcela when the latter flatters her and prevails upon their friendship in order to use Laura's room for her own purposes. Laura is intensely jealous and incredulous even though Félix declares he has abandoned Nise. She employs her imagination too much, and this is the basis of her jealousy. But she is adept at deception, as we have already seen.

Nise does not appear in the play and her sole function is to arouse Laura's jealousy and thus provide a conflict between herself and Félix. There are several pairs of friends for the mutual exchange of confidential problems: Félix and Lisardo, and Marcela and Laura; Félix, Marcela's brother, and Fabio, Laura's father, are the respective custodians of the girls' honor.

In this play Calderón dramatizes the personal mask which people wear to conceal their true sentiments for fear of violating conventions and traditions and of bringing dishonor upon themselves and their family. He shows us that once this mask is removed and the true feelings of the characters are made known, the manifold problems are easily solved. Some of the humor of the play derives from Calderón's mild satire of such social conventions as marriage and the seclusion of women. It was the custom for either the father or brother of the girl to arrange the marriage, but in the play Marcela takes the initiative in her love affair with Lisardo, and to a lesser extent Laura does the same in her romance with Félix.

The criticism most often leveled at the Cloak-and-Sword plays is that they lack profundity of theme and that all their brilliance is only superficial. It must be admitted that, while there is depth in the notion that one cannot be kept from or forced into a marriage either acceptable or repugnant to one's desires, it is overshadowed in the play by the intrigue, comic situations, the highly lyrical and baroque style and the clever interweaving of the action, all of which provide "good theater." Furthermore, the audience enjoys "being in" on the tricks and deceptions, and interest is maintained by its natural curiosity to ascertain the working out of the intrigue.

CHAPTER 6

The Costumbristic Plays

THE two outstanding plays usually assigned to the category of costumbristic drama (based partly on history, popular tradition or legend) are both recasts of pieces originally written by other authors: *The Bride of Gómez Arias* (*La niña de Gómez Arias*) by Vélez de Guevara and *The Mayor of Zalamea* (*El alcalde de Zalamea*) by Lope de Vega. We shall discuss the second of the two; it is one of Calderón's most admired plays.

I *The Mayor of Zalamea* (*El alcalde de Zalamea*)

Plot Summary—A wealthy peasant, Pedro Crespo, feels obliged to quarter in his house Don Alvaro, the captain of a regiment of Spanish troops. The captain bursts in on Crespo's daughter, Isabel, who has been closeted in the attic with a female companion. The commander of the regiment, Don Lope de Figueroa, arrives in time to end a quarrel between Crespo and the captain. Later, the captain ties up Crespo and abducts Isabel. After raping her, he abandons her in a forest where she is finally rescued by her brother Juan. After his appointment as Mayor of Zalamea, Crespo begs the captain on bended knee to marry Isabel, offering him all his wealth. When the captain refuses, Crespo orders him imprisoned. Don Lope charges that Crespo has no jurisdiction over the military and demands the captain's release. The King learns of the dispute and enters to hear the case. He is informed that the captain has been garroted and concludes that the King's justice has many instruments. The play ends as the King names Crespo perpetual Mayor of Zalamea.

Plot Structure—The main theme of *The Mayor of Zalamea* revolves about honor, which is contrasted with dishonor as it is dramatized in the first two acts where the dishonorable deeds of Captain Alvaro comprise the main action.[1] The themes of prudence and justice, which constitute Crespo's claim to fame, are developed primarily in the third act, although, of course, glimpses of them are interspersed throughout Acts One and Two and these virtues show a progressive development as the play unfolds. The secondary action deals with the jurisdictional dispute which arises when Crespo, the Mayor of Zalamea, and Lope, the old general, argue whether the civil authorities or the military should try the captain for his crimes. The secondary action, which reaches its height in Act Three—where it merges with the main action and becomes an integral part of it—has the roots of its later transformation in Acts One and Two.

The plot is a tightly-knit action of cause and effect. The basic causes of the conflict are: 1) the lodging of troops in a house where there is an unmarried female, Isabel, and 2) the curiosity of the captain over a beauty he is forbidden to see. The action is fast-moving, bristling with an abduction, a sexual assault, a garroting and a jurisdictional battle which can only be resolved peaceably by the King. The arrangement of the incidents is such that they develop from the previous ones, not only logically but also psychologically. Moreover, each act ends on a tide of mounting tension.

The major conflict is produced on two levels: the exterior and the interior. The essential ingredient in both involves rank or jurisdiction. The exterior conflict emerges from the clash between Crespo and Lope over the question of whether the King's justice is to be administered by the military or the civilian authorities. The interior conflict evolves from the decision Crespo must make as to whether he should act in his capacity as a father or as the newly elected Mayor of Zalamea. He finally chooses the latter because it embraces a wider sphere of justice than the personal.

The external conflicts are set forth as debates or arguments and encompass the theme of honor. In the first act Lope and Crespo argue over the disrespect the latter has shown to a captain. Crespo would slay an officer of even higher rank if he sullied his good reputation or that of his family. On the other hand, Lope is just as adamant in his insistence that nobody but himself may judge a member of the armed forces. Crespo's point is that his wealth and even his life are the possession of the King, but honor is the patrimony of the soul and the soul belongs only to God.

One of the most moving scenes of the play occurs when Crespo attempts to get the captain to marry Isabel in order to solve the honor problem. With tears in his eyes Crespo pleads his case, offering all his wealth to the captain and finally himself to serve as a slave. The fact that Crespo has acted first as a father to allow the culprit every opportunity to rectify the wrong he has committed and thus restore the family honor shows his humanity and his deep sense of justice. Another might have slain the captain at once, or might have made only a token appeal. But Crespo's impassioned plea has the ring of sincerity. At the same time that it exalts the character of Crespo in the mind of the audience, it also denigrates that of the captain when the latter not only refuses Crespo's generous offer but flaunts his arrogance in the old man's face, rashly refusing to recognize his authority as mayor. "Hope springs eternal in the human heart," and Crespo makes one final, desperate effort to avoid pronouncement of the extreme penalty upon the captain—capital punishment for rape. After the mayor reproaches him for his unbridled passion and orders his arrest, the captain reproves Crespo for his "excesses" and asks to be treated with "respect" because he is outside the realm of civilian authority. In one of the most biting passages of irony in Calderón's theater, Crespo hurls the theme of respect in the face of the captain, ordering that he be "respectfully" clapped in jail.

To bring together the two principals in the legal quarrel, Calderón has Lope confront Crespo. The former is beside himself with rage and threatens to use the army to back up his demands. The argument is expressed in short staccato-like dialogue, permeated with balanced phrases, queries, oaths, threats, counterthreats and boasting.

The climax is reached when open hostility is about to erupt between Lope and Crespo as the former storms the jail to free the captain. At that moment the King arrives; his timely appearance enables Calderón to solve the problem. The jurisdictional question is cleverly argued by Crespo, who maintains that both the military and civilian authorities are all part of the King's justice.

Style—The style, like the action, is simple, direct and straightforward. The picturesque patter of the low-life characters adds naturalness to the dialogue. The oaths of Rebolledo, a raw recruit, who curses the officer who forces the troops to march without rest or refreshment, parallel the curses of the stern regimental commander, Don Lope de Figueroa, whose painful gout makes him irritable and quarrelsome.

The argumentative aspect of the style has already been discussed in connection with the conflicts of the action. It is introduced early in the play when Rebolledo and La Chispa speak in terms of legal phraseology.

Calderón's Gongoristic style appears only once and then in a long soliloquy by Isabel bemoaning the calamity that has overtaken her. This lament has drawn the criticism that it lacks the simplicity, spontaneity and naturalness called for by the situation.[2] Since it is too long to be reproduced here, we can summarize it as a poetic depiction of Isabel's shame. She dreads the coming of dawn since its light will reveal the stain on her honor. She longs for the somber blackness of night to conceal her guilt, hopelessness and despair. The figures are appropriate to the outrage perpetrated by the captain on Isabel. Calderón was dealing with a delicate situation whose harshness he mitigated by cloaking Isabel's feelings in euphuistic terms.

Characterization—A basic idea of the play is the never-ending struggle between good and evil, rooted specifically in the unbridled passion of the malicious captain on the one hand, as opposed on the other to the broad humanity and the keen sense of justice of a prudent peasant. That the problem of an aristocrat who forces his attentions on a peasant girl was widespread and serious may be indicated by the frequency of its appearance in the theater of the time. Along with the polarity of good and evil represented by Crespo and the captain, there are numerous secondary characters portrayed in varying stages between these two extremes. Pedro Crespo, in accordance with the "law of subordination," is the protagonist around whom all the action revolves. It is he who influences most of the secondary characters: Don Mendo, whom he rejects as a son-in-law; Juan, whom he allows to enlist in the army because the lad has been too shiftless, and who, heeding his father's advice, unknowingly goes to help his dishonored sister; Don Alvaro, the captain, whom Crespo garrotes for the crimes of kidnapping and rape after the culprit has refused the chance to repair the damage; Isabel, who is forgiven by her father and because of his insistence is obliged to sign the deposition against the captain; Don Lope, who is compelled to admit Crespo's prudence; and finally the King, who accepts Pedro's concept of justice. The major clash between Crespo and the captain is mirrored by a secondary conflict between Crespo and Don Lope. The thematic common denominator is social justice. Is it right for a military nobleman to abduct and rape a peasant girl and, in the final analysis, does it matter which branch of the King's service redresses the injury as long as the cause of justice has been served?

The characterizations are outstanding for their attention to variety and to detail. Towering head and shoulders above the other personages is Pedro Crespo who represents justice and prudence. But while he symbolizes these two virtues, he is not a character lacking flesh and blood. Like every mortal he is endowed with some defects. As the soldiers of Lope's regiment enter Zalamea, one discusses the rumors about this rich peasant: "I have heard that he is the vainest man in the world, and that he is more pompous and presumptuous than a prince of León." On the other hand Crespo has a deep sense of honor and personal dignity together with a willingness to assume his social and civic responsibilities. In contrast to the attitude of his son who favors the purchase of a patent of nobility to exempt the family from the obligation of lodging the military, Crespo welcomes the opportunity to serve God and King. He is justly proud of his clear lineage and remarks that one cannot buy honor with money. Crespo's warmth and humanity are depicted in the scene where his son Juan leaves to join the regiment. Crespo doesn't want his son to be a lazy, good-for-nothing youth and hence has allowed him to join the army. After a poignant farewell the father sits in the open doorway of his house to watch his son disappear in the falling shadows of dusk.

The real mettle of Crespo's character is vividly shown in Act Two where the old father on bended knee before the captain is willing to give not only his entire estate, leaving nothing for his own son, but also his life and his son's to slavery in order to increase Isabel's dowry, if only the captain will marry her. Crespo boasts, and not without good reason, that he is respected and esteemed by his equals. Nobody gossips about him, nor reproaches him for being modest. He comes to symbolize not only prudence and justice, but also magnanimity, kindness and humility in varying degrees.

Captain Alvaro is the very antithesis of Pedro Crespo. Early in the first act we are given to understand that he is something of a Don Juan, since the sergeant has chosen Crespo's house for lodging the army officer primarily because of the mayor's beautiful daughter. But Alvaro despises peasant women; he only wants to marry one who is "immaculate and shapely." He is contumacious, proud, arrogant, vain and contemptuous of others. Isabel adequately summarizes his character in Act Two as "over-bearing, rash, discourteous, tyrannical and daring."

The gouty old general, Lope de Figueroa, is in a way a copy of Crespo. He is stubborn, proud but also just, thoughtful, considerate and prudent. After his argument with Crespo, he yields discerningly to superior reason. We first see Don Lope crossing verbal swords with Crespo over jurisdiction at the end of Act One when the mayor avers he would kill even a general if he sullied his honor as the captain has done. Don Lope prudently ejects the captain and decides to lodge in Crespo's house himself. He admits that Crespo was right and even that the mayor can curse as freely as he. The next time we see Don Lope is in Act Two where he is more relaxed. He again secretly admires Crespo's prudence in isolating his daughter from the soldiery. During the street brawl Lope at first hides his feelings to spare Crespo, but only momentarily, for the rage of both men bursts into open view over the insult to Crespo's honor by a member of the armed forces under Lope's command. Again Lope shows his prudence by ordering the captain and his men out of Zalamea. Before Lope leaves, he bids a touching farewell to Crespo and his family and hands Isabel a locket adorned with diamonds.

In Act Three Lope is much concerned over the disappearance from his regiment of Crespo's son, Juan, and returns to the village to ascertain what has happened. When Lope learns of the captain's imprisonment, the haughty general threatens to use the army to enforce his demands and even to set fire to the prison. In spite of his severity and irascibility, indeed, perhaps because of them, the general is respected by his own men.

Even the minor characters are artfully depicted with lifelike features. Mendo, the impoverished nobleman, seeks to marry Isabel primarily because he sees in the union a way to bolster his depleted purse. He is headstrong and impetuous when he knocks out some of Nuño's teeth in a fit of rage.

Rebolledo is a rogue like Mendo; both are interested only in financial gain. When things go wrong in the captain's plan to seduce Isabel, it is Rebolledo who blurts out the true state of affairs in order to save his own skin. La Chispa, his woman, is dynamic, loyal and sacrificial. In order to be near her lover, she has given up a life of comfort in exchange for the hardships of army life. She is not like other women who cry over the least little thing that goes wrong; La Chispa sings to keep up her spirits.

The sergeant, like his counterpart Nuño, is more realistic than his master and suggests that one cannot expect a girl to fall in love with one who is to leave on the morrow.

Juan's greatest weakness is gambling. He is easily fascinated by the army uniform and so joins the regiment with his father's consent. Like his father he shows discretion when he perceives the evil intent of the captain's ruse. He is the staunch defender of his sister's honor and is obedient to his father's instructions when he goes first to the aid of a woman in distress, little realizing that she is his own sister.

The Mayor of Zalamea stands out as a dramatic masterpiece because of its closely-knit plot construction, its life-like portrayal of both major and minor figures, the warmth of its humanity, its beautiful lyric verses, the loftiness of the themes, the intensity of its action, the skillful use of such technical devices as timing, tone, argumentation and dialectics, the naturalness of its dialogue, all of which blend into a perfect harmony and unity.

CHAPTER 7

The Religious Dramas

CALDERON has left a few more than a dozen religious plays. They contain not only much of the dramatist's ideology, but also many of the leitmotifs found in his secular dramas. Here one encounters a dramatization of various aspects of religion: the dogmas of the Church, legends relating to the image of the Madonna, the conversion of pagans to Christianity, the lives of saints and martyrs, the clash between good and evil, and stories from the Bible. There are several outstanding religious plays, and we have selected for discussion *Absalom's Hair* (*Los cabellos de Absalón*), which has not received the attention it merits, perhaps because it broaches the delicate theme of incest[1]; *The Constant Prince* (*El príncipe constante*); and *The Wonder-Working Magician* (*El mágico prodigioso*).

I *Absalom's Hair* (*Los cabellos de Absalón*)

Absalom's Hair is essentially a tragic drama about the passions of mankind—principally love and ambition, both of which, when perverted, lead man to misery and ultimate destruction. There are many subordinate motifs stemming from these two main themes. Love, for example, is seen in its various aspects: the filial love of Amón for David, the paternal love of David for his offspring, the incestuous love of Amón for Tamar, and finally the self-love of Absalón. Hate, the opposite of love, appears in at least two main personages: Absalón's hatred of his brother and father, and Tamar's later hatred of Amón and Jonadab. As a result of this hate, the revenge motif dominates when Tamar orders death for Jonadab. The same motif aids her role in the conspiracy in order to avenge her outraged honor, and also when Absalón plans Amón's death. The opposite of revenge is forgiveness, and this motif is found only in David, who pardons his erring children and Joab and Semeí.

Plot Summary—Amón, one of King David's children, is in love with his half-sister, Tamar. Urged on by the advice of a false friend, Jonadab, Amón yields to his passion and has incestuous relations with Tamar.

Absalón, another son of David, has ambitions of becoming king. To satisfy his lust for power, he will go to any extreme, even slaying his brothers and father, if need be. Tamar's seduction provides Absalón with the excuse he needs to plot the death of his strongest rival for the throne, Amón.

With his father's knowledge, Absalón invites Amón and his brothers Salomón, Adonías and also Tamar to a banquet at the family estate in Baalhasor. Under the pretext of revenge for the stain to Tamar's honor, Absalón slays Amón.

Obliged by others who force him to practice the love he preaches, David pardons Absalón. The latter considers his father to be senile because he was moved by love rather than by justice. Aquitofel, a conspirator with Absalón and others against David, urges Absalón to adopt a more extreme policy and resort to open warfare. Absalón plans to enlarge his forces before declaring war.

The prophetess Teuca predicts that the friendship between David and Absalón will soon break out into open hostility. She prophesies cryptically that Aquitofel will find a rope. He chooses to interpret the prophecy as signifying a judgeship for him, not realizing that the prophecy really means his death. Cusay, a faithful follower of David, reproves Aquitofel for misguiding Absalón, and urges a more moderate course of action. Later, rejected by Absalón, Aquitofel hangs himself.

As the conflict between David and Absalón grows more intense, the King, still under the influence of love, advises one of his generals, Joab, not to harm the rebellious prince. As Absalón rides through the forest, his long hair is caught in the low branches of the trees and he is left hanging between heaven and earth. Violating David's order, Joab pierces the dangling body with a spear to make sure the prince is dead, realizing that only by Absalón's demise will peace and tranquility be restored to the kingdom.

Plot Structure—The plot structure rests on two actions: the principal action deals with Absalón's vaunting ambition to become king, and the secondary action concerns Amón's rape of Tamar. The two actions are linked thematically by the element of passion—a lust of the flesh and a lust for power. The secondary action is the spark which ignites the main action. The former has its source in the play by Tirso de Molina, *The Vengeance of Tamar* (*La venganza de Tamar*), and derives ultimately from the Bible, *II Samuel,* 13. Calderón lifted his second act almost verbatim from Tirso's play where it functions as Act Three. Calderón's play has a much broader sweep than Tirso's since the former involves more of David's family in the action. Moreover, in Calderón's work the secondary action moves in a limited sphere reaching its climax at the end of Act Two. The main action, which has its roots in the first and second acts, blossoms forth in Act Three and succeeds in surpassing the secondary action in emotional and dramatic intensity as Calderón depicts the downfall of a house divided against itself.

Techniques—One of the more interesting techniques that Calderón employs to highlight an event or force a character to act or react is indirect illumination.

Posing as a widow in mourning, Teuca complains of her misfortune: one of her two sons has killed the other. A court has decreed that she hand over the guilty son she is hiding, or die. David rules that "the one who pardons accomplishes more than the one who takes vengeance." In this way, Teuca indirectly forces David to practice what he preaches as his philosophy of life. Seeing his own problems reflected in Teuca's, the King feels obliged to pardon Absalón for slaying Amón.

Character Portrayal—The characters of the play are a strange assortment of selfish and even psychotic figures easily induced to commit horrible acts. Indeed, it may well have been the author's intent to show that the sins of the fathers are visited upon the children. David's immoral life in the pre-stage action (homicide and adultery) in regard to Uriah and Bathsheba respectively will be reflected in that of his children, Tamar, Amón and Absalón.

Amón suffers from an unrestrained imagination. Under the influence of his servant Jonadab, Amón follows the suggestion that he violate his half-sister, Tamar. Through Jonadab's suggestion, he creates in his mind the desire for illicit sexual relations. Amón realizes that his love for Tamar is wrong, but he rationalizes that it is a part of his destiny. The prince does not face the problem directly but obliquely. He conceals his passion for Tamar under the guise of love for another woman whom the princess resembles. Since he is somewhat timid about declaring his love, he asks Tamar to *play* the role of his lady-love during a rehearsal so he can overcome his bashfulness. She agrees, if it will relieve his pain.

Amón knows exactly what he is doing when he begs David to allow Tamar to bring him food. He also knows that the nourishment he needs is genuine love. Nevertheless, he persists only in consummating a carnal love affair. He is also easily influenced by sensory appeals (food and music) and by the suggestions of Jonadab.

Tamar is portrayed as a "sympathetic" half-sister, who out of naïveté or pity agrees to play the role of sweetheart to Amón to After she discovers that it was Jonadab who had urged Amón to seduce her, she vengefully favors punishment for him. Later, she is shown to be something of an opportunist when she comes to the aid of Absalón in gathering additional reinforcements for his campaign against his father and his brothers.

Absalón is proud, arrogant, and a deceiver. His lust for power drives him to slay Amón, his foremost rival for the throne of David. He condemns Joab for his pride but fails to perceive the same fault in himself. He edges toward a persecution complex since he believes that Joab is always opposing him. He finds justification in his ambition to obtain the throne because he judges that his father has been "blinded" by family love in pardoning Amón.

Absalón's deceit is manifested in his statement to David that "nobody in Israel loves Amón more than I." His "love" for Amón is in reality a cloak for his hatred. He admits to Aquitofel that his reconciliation with his father is feigned and was effected for the purpose of obtaining David's good will. Like Amón he sometimes faces a crisis indirectly by hiding the real motives for his conduct. Under the pretext of removing the stain to Tamar's honor, he slays his brother.

Just as Absalón has misinterpreted the whole purpose of his life, so he misinterprets the prophecy of the witch, Teuca, who foretells that his ambition will cause him to be held aloft by his hair. Absalón considers this to mean he will be king since his hair is his crowning glory. But in truth it of course presages his death by hanging.

The figure of David moves in a world of paternal love. In his concern over Amón's melancholy, he does not question his son's motives in requesting permission that Tamar be allowed to serve him food. Later he expresses great mental anguish over Tamar's violation. His dilemma is marked by a conflict of interests: shall he administer justice as a king, or shall he show love as a father? Rationalizing that pardon is better than punishment, David forgives Absalón for slaying Amón. He does this not only out of love but also in deference to public opinion. He warns his general, Joab, to see to it that no harm befalls Absalón.

Aquitofel, an adviser of Absalón and his fellow conspirator against David, is shrewd, ambitious and self-seeking. He proposes a delay in the attempted coup d'état until Absalón has added more followers to his cause. He plays David against Absalón and vice versa in his attempt to obtain a judgeship. Like Absalón, he misinterprets the witch Teuca's prophecy that he will find a rope. For him it signifies the coveted judgeship; in reality it portends his death. He hangs himself in Act Three when Absalón deflates his ego by rejecting his advice.

Several other minor characters like the faithful servant to David, old Cusay, Salomón, another ambitious candidate for the throne, and Jonadab, the false friend of Amón, round out a gallery of strange personages.

Imagery—The images are geared to the themes of lust of the flesh and the lust for power; their interrelationship adds another link of unity to the work. They appeal to the senses of sight, hearing and taste. The first set of images we shall consider are those dealing with food, which Calderón associates with sex. In Act One Amón with the aid of his servant Jonadab succeeds in convincing David by the use of food metaphors to allow Tamar to bring him something to eat. In the banquet scene of Act Two after Amón discovers the identity of the veiled Tamar whom he has violated, his "love" turns to loathing: "I did not expect to find such an aperitif," and he leaves in disgust. With ominous portents, Tamar cries after him, "You will get a worse dessert . . . your last plate will be the vengeance of Tamar." In the last scene of Act Two as the lifeless body of Amón lies draped across the table, Absalón delivers the eulogy, "for you, dear brother, this invitation has been prepared; this plate, although laden with thankless food, has satisfied our hurt. May it do you some good. Drink the blood, Tamar."

Another set of images relates Absalón's insatiable passion to govern with food imagery. When he discovers the crown on a platter, he remarks, "if it is so savory to rule, as the ambitious one affirms, then such a morsel is not to be foregone."

Several other images merit a word of comment. After the seduction when Amón scorns Tamar, the latter refers to her seducer in gambling terminology. Reproachfully she calls him a "gambler of her honor." Tamar then speaks of the "rake-off," "winnings," and "losses."

Floral imagery plays a significant role in the work. Teuca, the prophetess, arrives with a basket of flowers which represent an image of *love* with reference to Tamar. She refuses to accept them, for the flower of virginity which matters most to her has been lost. The symbolism of the different flowers which Teuca distributes to the four princes is in harmony with the theme of love, or with its perversion as this applies to each of them. Amón draws two flowers, the lily, and the cat-tail. The former symbolizes the purity of Tamar which he has violated, and the latter may be either a phallic symbol, or a sign of the justice which will soon overtake Amón. Adonías receives a larkspur which often harms, and he is advised to beware of courting a married woman. The laurel wreath is given to Salomón with the warning that he may be ruined by "flowers of love" if he courts women in his old age. Absalón gets the narcissus, which represents self-love, and which will destroy him.

Absalom's Hair is one of the most eventful and moving tragedies in Calderón's theater. The true tragedy lies not in the death of Absalón, who deserved to die, but in the mental anguish of

David who must suffer the heartbreak of a father over the children's sins which are in a way a reflection of his own wicked life.

II *The Constant Prince* (*El príncipe constante*)

Plot Summary—Act One. As the play opens, Fénix, a beautiful Moorish princess, is very unhappy because her father, the King of Fez, wants her to marry a man she does not love, Tarudante, King of Morocco. She is in love with one Muley who is distressed and jealous when he sees the princess looking at a picture of Tarudante which her father has given her. A nephew of the King of Fez, and a general in his army, Muley has returned from the North African coast with the news that a large armada of Portuguese troops is about to invade Tangiers.

Two Portuguese princes, Fernando and Enrique, are disembarking their troops. Enrique falls and considers it an omen which foreshadows a catastrophe. His pessimistic attitude is in sharp contrast to Fernando's undying faith in the ultimate success of the expedition.

In an encounter with some Moors Fernando captures Muley, but upon hearing of his love affair, he sets his prisoner free. In gratitude Muley swears to be Fernando's slave eternally. Soon afterwards, the Portuguese are surrounded by Moorish troops and Fernando becomes the prisoner of the King of Fez who sends Enrique back to Portugal to obtain ransom money.

Act Two. Fénix relates to Muley the dream she had while resting in the woods after a walk. In it she was seized by an old hag who prophesied that she would be "the price of a dead one." Muley misinterprets the prediction, thinking he will lose her to Tarudante.

Fernando urges his fellow captives to endure imprisonment with patience. News of the death of the Portuguese King, Duarte, saddens the Christian captives. The provisions of his will that the city of Ceuta be ceded in exchange for Fernando is rejected by the prince who prefers to be a slave of the King of Fez but constant to the Catholic faith. The King demands unquestioning obedience from Fernando, but the latter refuses to surrender Ceuta. Muley, because he owes his life and freedom to Fernando, vows to repay the debt.

The King puts Fernando to work in Fénix's garden where the

Prince encourages other Christian captives to be prudent and brave. Fernando brings flowers to Fénix and when she asks who is to be the dead one, the prince answers "I," because "man is born to be subject to fortune and death."

When the King sees Muley and Fernando speaking, he suspects something afoot. To place the responsibility of Fernando's captivity squarely on Muley's shoulders, the monarch entrusts the prince to his keeping. Fernando advises Muley to serve the King as he cannot accept freedom if he must also sully his friend's honor.

Act Three. Muley and, later, Fénix appear before the King to plead Fernando's case. The King points out that Fernando is cruel to himself, for it is in his hands to cede Ceuta.

Don Alfonso, King of Portugal, arrives with money and jewels as a ransom for Fernando but the King of Fez refuses to release his royal prisoner except in exchange for the city of Ceuta. When the King of Morocco offers his heart to Fénix, the King of Fez orders Muley to guard Tarudante's future wife. For a second time Muley faces a dilemma over a conflict of interest.

Another test of Fernando's constancy occurs when he is about to die of starvation since the King has forbidden his people to provide sustenance. Fernando underscores man's inhumanity to man by pointing out how there is pity among animals but not among men. As Fernando, ever loyal to the Catholic faith, is near death, the religious aspect of the play moves to the forefront. Bearing a lighted candle and garbed in the mantle of his order, Fernando guides the Portuguese troops to victory. After Fernando's death, Alfonso offers Fénix, who had been captured previously along with Muley and Fernando, in exchange for the corpse. If the King refuses, Fénix will be killed. The King demurs and Alfonso offers his living captives (Fénix, Muley and Tarudante) for the dead body of Fernando, asking only that Muley marry Fénix. The curtain falls as the soldiers bear Fernando's coffin to a waiting ship.

The première performance of *The Constant Prince* was probably given on February 23, 1629 by the company of Bartolomé Romero.[2] The play contained some satirical verses directed against the Gongoristic sermons preached by the court chaplain, Fray Hortensio Paravicino. Actually the cleric was inveighing against the outrages perpetrated against some nuns by actors and poets who seemed to be encouraging disturbances.

In a quarrel among theatrical people near the convent of the Trinitarian nuns in Madrid, an actor, Pedro de Villegas, wounded Calderón's brother and fled, taking refuge in the nunnery. Calderón, the police and a noisy crowd of followers forced their way into the convent and when the culprit could not be found, subjected the sisters to insults and rough treatment.

Among the nuns was Lope de Vega's daughter, Marcela, who had professed in 1623 at the age of seventeen. The scandal provoked the wrath of Fray Hortensio who on January 11, 1629 had preached a memorial sermon in honor of the deceased parents of Philip IV. He took advantage of the occasion to chide actors and dramatic poets for fomenting disorders in the capital.

At that time Calderón was writing *The Constant Prince,* and he put into the mouth of the clown, Brito, some Gongoristic verses aimed at Paravicino. After returning safely from a sea voyage in which there had been danger of shipwreck, Brito the clown jokes about his arrival on dry land and prays that he may never suffer death by drowning. Then he remarks:

A funeral oration is forged
which is a sermon in jibberish:
it is a panegyric which I tell to the water,
and I complain in Hortensian drivel
because my anger, springing from watered wine
remains and it is now old.

(Una oración se fragua
fúnebre, que es sermón de Berbería:
panegírico es que digo al agua,
y en emponomio horténsico me quejo;
porque este enojo, desde que se fragua
con ella el vino, me quedó, y ya es viejo.)

Paravicino lodged a complaint and Calderón was confined to house arrest for several days. Finally the objectionable verses were ordered deleted but not before they had been recited for several days for the public including a performance before the King.[3]

The above information is valuable to help us date the composition of the play. H. W. Hilborn assigned the date 1629 to *The Constant Prince*.[4] Since time was needed for rehearsals, it seems more likely that the play was composed toward the end of 1628.

Sources—Professor Sloman has devoted a book to tracing the sources both remote and immediate of *The Constant Prince*.[5] The remote source is the Portuguese expedition against Tangiers in 1437 as it has been recorded by João Alvaro, the biographer of Fernando, in his *Chronicle*, preserved in manuscript form in the Biblioteca Nacional at Madrid and edited by Mendes dos Remédios in Coimbra, 1911. In 1579, one Hieronymo de Ramos published an emended second edition (there is no extant copy of the first printed edition of 1527) which contains a chapter (not found in the manuscript) dealing with the return of Fernando's body to Portugal. But five years before, Camoens had already included such an episode in the fourth canto of his epic poem, *Os Lusíadas*. It seems, then, that the chroniclers accepted as fact the poet's interpolation of the Regulus episode which was later repeated by other historians and found its way into a play attributed to Lope de Vega and entitled *The Adverse Fortune of Prince Fernando of Portugal* (*La fortuna adversa del Infante Don Fernando de Portugal*), the immediate source of Calderón's play. Another was the *Epitome of Portuguese Histories* (*Epítome de las historias portuguesas*) written by one Manuel de Faria y Sousa and published in 1628. This history with its great emphasis on the personal tragedy of Fernando served in part as a source of inspiration for Calderón.

The action of the play is carried by means of two triangles. The main action is a pseudo-love triangle in which Fernando and the King of Fez clash over their "love" for the city of Ceuta. The triangle of the sub-plot concerns the love of Muley and Tarudante for Fénix. The unifying theme in both is constancy: in the first it is Fernando's constancy to his religious beliefs; in the second it is Fénix's faithfulness to Muley.

As other critics have pointed out (discussed in the next section), Ceuta is equated with Fénix. Both are associated with the idea of beauty. Since Muley courts Fénix and refuses to surrender her to Tarudante, and Fernando prefers to die rather than to give up Ceuta, there is thus established a thematic nexus between the two actions. In order to avoid detracting from the importance of the main action, Calderón leaves much of the sub-plot undeveloped.

The play opens with the sub-plot of romantic action. Imbedded in it is the relationship between Muley, a Moorish general, and the Christian captive, Fernando, which will in part weld the two actions together. Like a Christian caballero, Muley aided a Portuguese ship in distress. Furthermore, he expresses his jealousy over seeing a picture of his rival, Tarudante, in the hands of his ladylove, Fénix. He anticipates the main action by announcing the landing of Portuguese troops in North Africa.

The two plots are also intertwined through the relationship between Fernando and Muley. The Portuguese prince captures Muley, but on hearing of his love affair, he releases him. Grateful, Muley promises to aid Fernando in the future. Muley's capture will be paralleled by Fernando's imprisonment later by the King of Fez. The humanity of the Portuguese prince will be contrasted with the inhumanity and cruelty of the Moorish King.

More specific examples of the linkage can be seen in Act Two. Fénix has related the account of her dream that she would be the price of a dead man. It is misinterpreted by Muley who thinks the reference is to himself since he would rather die than allow Fénix to marry Tarudante. The interlacing of the two actions becomes even more apparent in the scene of the two complementary sonnets on the flowers (uttered by Fernando) and the stars (recited by Fénix) where even the imagery is merged:

> for if one day is the lifetime of the flowers,
> one night is the age of the stars.

The fate of the two is linked by the ill fortune of one and the impending death of the other. Since the King of Fez demands the surrender of Ceuta, a price Prince Fernando is not willing to pay for his freedom, the Portuguese prince, who is in reality a slave, prefers to die and is in fact figuratively dead. When Fénix asks who the dead person is to be, Fernando enters at the propitious moment and declares "I."

Another link in the chain connecting the two plots is forged through the responsibility given to Muley by the King of Fez. Muley is put in charge of Fernando after the King has seen them talking secretly together and suspects something amiss (Act Two). Moreover, the King also asks Muley to guard Fénix, the future wife of Tarudante (Act Three). Muley is in a dilemma; Fernando suggests a way out: be faithful to the King, for he is above everyone else. In the hierarchy of values, love and friendship are inferior to loyalty and honor. In the meantime Fernando will be a constant prince to his God and his religion even in the servitude of Fez.

The ending is moving and theatrical. Before Fernando expires, he wishes his remains to be placed in a church sepulchre, since he has founded so many churches for the glory of God. He has won eternity (honor and glory) through his actions; now he wants the memory of his image left in some physical form (as a tomb in a church) for posterity. Garbed in the mantle of his religious order, Fernando guides Alfonso's army to victory.

When Alfonso exchanges the prisoners, including Fénix, for the corpse of Fernando, the Moorish princess realizes the full import of the words: "I am to be the price of a dead man." Fernando's coffin is lowered from the walls and accompanied to the waiting armada by drums and trumpets as the Christian captives watch in silent and reverent awe.

Two of the earliest interpretations of the play were published together under the title "Calderón's *El príncipe constante:* Two Appreciations." [6] For Professor Wilson the "point" of the play is that the man who sincerely persists in his beliefs to the end is superior to his fellow human beings. Fernando is not only a Christian *soldier,* he is also a *gentleman* who sets Muley free when he is touched by the Moor's love story. He is a chivalrous man of action who may develop into a saint.

The King of Fez, the antagonist, is only cruel when his will has been thwarted. Like Fernando he too is actuated by high motives, and there is no rancor shown toward those of another religion. The struggle resolves itself basically into a conflict of two wills over the city of Ceuta. Enrique (the historical Prince Henry the Navigator) is a foil to Fernando. When he stumbles and falls, he considers it an ill omen that forebodes the failure of the expedition. Fernando chides him for his superstition, but the omen serves a dramatic function in creating an atmosphere of impending doom. It also stresses the difference between a strong prince and a weak one.

Muley is depicted as a typical hero of a palace play. He is a conventional figure who possesses all of Fernando's military virtues of loyalty and friendship.

Fénix suffers from melancholia because her father wishes her to marry Tarudante against her will. Furthermore, she is much upset over the old woman's prophecy, which she thinks refers to Muley. Like Enrique's fall on landing in Africa, it is an omen of misfortune.

The two contrasting sonnets on flowers and stars in Act Two reveal the different attitudes of Fernando and Fénix—they both see the changing fortune of men reflected in the brief life of the flowers and stars. In the face of death Fernando bears the brevity of life stoically. On the other hand, Fénix is afraid of death and lacks the Christian's fortitude to overcome her fears.

According to Professor Wilson, the play shows how a good man becomes a saint. The figure of Fernando represents any man who sacrifices himself and all he holds dear for his beliefs.

Professor Entwistle views the play as a great symbolic drama, a kind of *auto sacramental*. Behind the characters manipulated by the author, there is the clash between good and evil. It is more than a historical play, it is in fact powerful religious drama in which a prince who fails to achieve a victory in life leads his army in death to a great spiritual victory. As in all symbolic drama, eternal and abstract values appear to collide with material and mundane forces. Prince Fernando symbolizes Constancy or Fortitude or simply Faith—a Faith that is opposed to Human Understanding as represented by Enrique. Human Understanding has its shortcomings; it may judge more accurately over the short view of things, but it may fail in the long run.

The King of Fez, being an infidel, represents tyranny, possessing power illegally. Fénix is a symbol of Beauty. Melancholic, she soon realizes her worthlessness and that she will be exchanged for a dead man. Beauty, like time, soon passes, and it is this harrowing thought which crosses Fénix's mind and permeates the entire play. Both men and women are subject to death and the whims of Fortune.

Professor Sloman interprets the play as a dramatization for the virtue of fortitude as defined by St. Thomas Aquinas in the *Summa Theologica,* II, ii, QQ, cxxiii-cxxxix.[7] Fortitude, which ranks third after Prudence and Justice, is made up of an aggressive side (doing good) and an enduring side (the endurance of suffering and evil). Its main characteristic of endurance is the aspect which seems to have been uppermost in Calderón's mind when he wrote the play.

Professor Wardropper takes issue with the interpretations set forth by the three critics previously cited.[8] He is of the opinion that Wilson's close reading of the text does not necessarily lead the reader to the author's intended meaning of the play. He finds the approach developed by Entwistle and Sloman too schematic and their methods unacceptable. The play must be studied, he argues, from the viewpoint of two worlds separated by a deep chasm in ideology: the Christian and the Moorish. The gap is bridged on a worldly and sentimental level by love and the threat to one's beloved. Both Christian and Moor experience sentiment, but only Fernando, the Christian, feels the sufferings of other people. This is the essential difference between Muley, the good, and Fernando, the aspirant to saintliness.

Both Muley and Fernando are constant in their own way. Muley is the constant suitor of Fénix, the constant friend of Fernando and the constant subject of the King of Fez. Thus Muley has some understanding on a religious level of Fernando's constancy to his beliefs in the Christian faith.

The ransom which the Moors demand for Fernando is Ceuta, the Christian city, which in Calderón's mind represents Beauty. In the Hebrew tongue Ceuta means "beauty." Now it is a Christian city, beautiful in the eyes of the Catholic faith. When the Moors ask for the city, they are asking for an exchange in beauty—worldly beauty for religious beauty. What actually takes place is an exchange of a mundane beauty (Fénix) for the spiritual beauty of Fernando's soul (his corpse is ephemeral).

In the conflicting set of values, the Moor emphasizes love and friendship; the Christian, loyalty and honor. The Christian's standard of values is founded on the assumption that the spiritual is of greater worth than the transient. The two complementary sonnets spoken by Fernando and Fénix in Act Two show how Calderón's concept of time is associated with different moral values. Time for the Moor is the measurement of love, feeling and friendship. But for the Christian, only eternity, or timelessness, is the dimension of honor, loyalty and constancy in faith. Since no man knows the exact moment of his death, time is equated with fortune or chance, which is unpredictable. But the Christian with his hope of eternal life considers death a release from the shackles of time. Temporality with its attendant cares, anxieties and unhappiness is of the world; timelessness or eternity is the possession of God, but Fernando's merging of his own sufferings with those of his fellow captives is his sacrificial self-effacement, his oblation to God in which he exchanges his temporal life for the life immortal of saintliness.

Y. Gulsoy and J. H. Parker regard the play as an expression of the preoccupations of the period.[9] They point out that other plays by Calderón treat of other burning issues of the day in the religious field. They cite his *The Great Prince of Fez* (which deals with the dogma of the Immaculate Conception); *The Devotion to the Cross* and *The Purgatory of St. Patrick* (the last two discuss the problem of predestination); and *The Wonder-Working Magician* (treating of an All-Powerful Deity).

According to Gulsoy and Parker, Calderón dramatizes the idea of martyrdom—a common manifestation of baroque artistic expression especially in painting. Examples given are Ribera's "St. Jerome"; Valdés Leal's "The Temptation of St. Anthony"; and Zurbarán's "St. Francis of Assisi."

Fernando must suffer martyrdom in order to exalt the Catholic faith. Speaking to the obdurate King of Fez, he warns:

> You will not triumph over the Church,
> Triumph over me, if you will;
> God will defend my cause
> Since I defend His.
>
> (Act Three)

The Christian prince cannot surrender to the infidel "a city which confesses God in the Catholic faith." Firm in the Catholic religion,

Fernando enumerates the virtues of his faith: long-suffering, patience, fortitude and endurance in adversity, torture and even death. The vigorous and spirited expression of his loyalty to the Catholic faith and his defense of the Church was the ideal and aspiration of the Counter Reformation. The "heroic element" and the "tragic dynamism," important features of baroque style studied by A. L. Constandse,[10] combined with the theme of martyrdom, could be interpreted only by that great religious spirit, Calderón de la Barca.

Disagreeing with Sloman who asserts that Fénix is exchanged for Fernando's corpse in order to humiliate beauty, William M. Whitby shows how important her role is in the ransoming of Fernando's remains.[11] First, Whitby reminds us that during the period of the Reconquest it was common among Moors to refer to cities metaphorically as beautiful women. He cites the well-known ballad of *Abenámar* in which the poet courts the city of Granada. Whitby next contends that the real significance of Fénix's role must be considered from the Christian rather than the Moorish point of view.

Fénix not only symbolizes Beauty by representing the city of Ceuta; her name also suggests eternal life since the mythological phoenix is supposed to rise from its own ashes. Toward the end of Act Three, Alfonso refers to Fénix as "a divine image," thus strengthening the idea that she is of great value. Since the city of Ceuta belongs to God it cannot be given as a ransom. But Fénix can be exchanged for Fernando's body and hence this interchange "symbolizes the transcendental recognition by Ceuta, through heaven's intercession, of her obligation to Fernando. It symbolizes Ceuta's act of surrendering herself, through heaven, on behalf of Fernando's spirit, thereby freeing his body from captivity. This is heaven's homage to the martyr, manifested in the physical world to which his body is chained by reason of its nature."

Carlos Ortigoza Vieyra in an analysis of the play's motives sees Fernando impelled by a chivalric spirit in the early scenes.[12] His sword is at the command of God; personal vanity does not appear in his actions but rather nobility of spirit, reason and valor in the face of danger. Fernando's every word and attitude reflect different aspects of the same motives: intelligence, temperance and faith. When he captures Muley, he is later motivated by commiseration, clemency, compassion and the freedom to choose the greatest moral good.

During his captivity, Fernando is motivated by his constancy in his faith, a strong will tested at every moment by vexations and sickness. Like Job he bears his burdens stoically; he feels pain and tries hard to suppress it. He sacrifices mundane honor for the divine. His captors make him suffer dishonor and humiliation which he endures patiently, motivated by a high standard of values.

The final interpretation we shall consider is that offered by the late Professor Spitzer concerning the figure of Fénix.[13] His study springs from two points of disagreement he had with Wolfgang Kayser ("Zur Struktur des *Standhaften Prinzen*," in *Gestaltprobleme der Dichtung* [Bonn, 1957]). Spitzer thinks that Fénix is more than the incarnation of worldly beauty, and that she is indeed placed in relation to the Constant Prince. His analysis, though based largely on the garden scene in which the two recite their famous sonnets on the flowers and stars, proceeds from a study of her appearance throughout the entire play.

Spitzer does not consider Muley to be the great love of Fénix but rather that their love is merely attachment for each other that dates from childhood because of the proximity of their houses. Muley was more in love with Fénix than she was with him. When Fernando releases Muley, he sends him as a gift or slave to a lady he does not yet know. This action foreshadows the possibility of what actually happens later but in a different sense, viz., that Fernando may become her "slave."

To Spitzer the expressions "price" and "ransom" connote "moral equivalents." Fernando's question concerns the value of his constancy in relation to Ceuta. Was it equal? Fénix's problem concerns her beauty. Was it equal in value to Fernando's constancy? For Spitzer the answer to both these questions is in the negative. Ceuta's value is far more than Fernando, but since he persists in his steadfastness to his ideals, his value increases more than Fénix's beauty.

When Fernando answers "I" to Fénix's question concerning "Who will this dead man be?" his reply suggests that she belongs to him; it reveals "an inner relationship with the princess and at the same time an acceptance of their fate of eternal separation in death."

Spitzer is convinced of an amorous relationship between Fernando and Fénix because of the former's use of the familiar forms. The flowers offered by the prince are not only a symbol of life and love, but also of death, since they wilt so quickly. Looking at the marigold (*maravilla*), Fénix puns with the name, classifying it as a miracle. After demolishing two other possible interpretations, Spitzer gathers the sense to be that "it is a miracle when Fernando, although destined to die, renders homage to her in bringing flowers lovingly." He finds the reference to the prince's decline "proof of Fénix's previous acquaintance with him. She has understood the dead man's wooing." The stichomythic dialogue between the two contains another important piece of evidence Spitzer adduces to show how Fénix experiences the woes of another in herself for the first time. Her line is: "You give me sorrow" (*"Pena das."*).

Fernando's flowers are hieroglyphs of his fate. Fénix sees her own fate in them also and is upset over the prospect of being separated from her lover. She is melancholic because she lacks something which Fernando has: constancy to his ideals in the face of adversity. For Fénix the stars represent the "changeable and the unforeseeable." The stars are equal to the flowers because both exert their influence on human destiny.

In searching for other evidence to support his hypothesis of a meeting and separation of lovers, Spitzer cannot imagine a purely "abstract confrontation between man and woman" on the stage without some bond of love joining them. Moreover, it had been a familiar theme since medieval days for a Christian knight to court a Moorish princess.

The familiar form which Fernando had used to Fénix in Act Two gives way in Act Three to the more polite forms to indicate a cooling in their relationship. Fernando comes to realize that Fénix's physical beauty is far from matched by the beauty of her soul when he observes her selfishness. Fénix cannot bear the sight of the ailing prince now on the threshold of death from starvation. When Fernando reproves her for not looking at him, Spitzer concludes that there must have been some previous intimacy between the two to provoke the prince to comment, "You do not even look at me!" He sees this as a bitter farewell, Fernando's painful disillusion over the decline in her moral value, and Fénix's realization that she is confronted with a hopeless situation.

Finally, in the resolution, since Fénix's value is not rated very high, not even in the eyes of her own father who is willing to let her die, she plus Muley and Tarudante are the ransom offered by the Christians for Fernando's remains. Moreover, Fénix marries Muley, not so much out of love but because of his relationship with Fernando. Spitzer concludes about the figure of Fénix, "She, who could not love, has no right to a will of her own, or to a real life."

III *The Wonder-Working Magician* (*El mágico prodigioso*)

The last religious play we shall consider is *The Wonder-Working Magician,* the so-called "Faust" play of the Spanish theater.

Plot Summary—Act One. Cipriano, a student, prefers to study his books in his search for truth while his two servants Clarín and Moscón attend a festival in nearby Antioch. The two servants, who also serve as the clowns of the play, are in love with Livia, the servant of Justina. Cipriano has been reading Pliny's *Historia naturalis* in order to form a concept of the true God. He is about to contemplate the hidden truth when the Devil disguised as a traveler en route to Antioch on business appears and engages him in a scholastic debate. Satan ironically defines God as the Highest Good, Unity, Omniscience, and Omnipotence. The Devil loses the argument when he cannot answer Cipriano's conclusion that such a God must be all-powerful. The Prince of Darkness decides to bring about Cipriano's ruin by making him forget his religious studies and fall victim to a feminine beauty.

Cipriano halts a duel between two pagan friends, Lelio, the governor's son, and Floro over Justina, a Christian. Both suitors aspire to her hand in marriage and, to settle the argument, Cipriano will visit her to ascertain which one she prefers.

In a long flashback we learn that Lisandro, a Christian, brought up Justina after her mother's death as a Christian martyr. Justina is angered by the festival celebrating the dedication of a temple to the pagan god Jupiter. When Cipriano relates the purpose of his visit, he too falls in love with Justina, but she rejects all proposals of marriage.

Floro and Lelio enter separately to court Justina. The Devil enters to defame her virtue and to arouse jealousy in the two suitors. Cipriano interrupts a duel for the second time between Floro and Lelio. He decides to abandon his books and studies and to pursue love.

Act Two. Justina rebukes Cipriano for persevering in his courtship. She informs him prophetically that it is impossible for her to love him until after death. In a soliloquy Cipriano is so carried away by his passion that he declares he would give his soul in exchange for Justina. Accompanied by thunder and lightning, the Devil in yet another disguise accepts Cipriano's offer to sell his soul. He promises to teach Cipriano a magic that will enable him to obtain anything he wants.

Lelio boldly enters Justina's apartment in his effort to ascertain the identity of the man (the Devil) he saw leaving her balcony on a previous occasion. The Devil enters again, vowing to stir up the greatest scandal in the household. Lisandro returns home unexpectedly and Justina asks Lelio to hide. As Lisandro is revealing to Justina his concern over the Emperor's decree against Christians, which the governor has just received, Floro also arrives to ascertain the identity of the man on the balcony (the Devil). In the ensuing conversation between Floro and Justina, Lelio realizes that the unknown lover could not have been Floro. When Floro alludes to the fact that Lelio is the governor's son and that Justina was attracted by his power, Lelio emerges and engages Floro in another duel. The governor arrives in time to stop the duel and order the arrest of the two.

Lisandro now finishes the story of Justina's parents he had begun in Act One. Her father killed her mother when he found out she was a Christian. Now Lisandro, who has brought her up as a Christian, condemns her for the scandal she has stirred up in his house.

The Devil shows Cipriano some examples of his power including a vision of Justina sleeping. Cipriano signs an agreement in blood to take lessons in black magic from the Devil. With his newly acquired power Cipriano hopes to win the love of Justina and be the terror of the world.

Act Three. Cipriano boasts in a soliloquy that he has become so expert in black magic that he can teach his master something. The Devil in an aside admits he cannot force Justina's will, only incline it. To this end Satan calls on all nature to sing of love in order to inflame Justina with passion. When Justina feels the pull of love, she becomes alternately upset and calm. When the Devil tries to tempt her, she calls on the name of God and is able to resist the power of Satan.

In the forest Cipriano is frustrated because his magic is unable to produce Justina. Finally a figure appears; Cipriano takes it to be Justina, but when he pulls aside the cloak, it turns out to be a skeleton which remarks:

> Thus Cipriano
> are all the glories of the world.

Disillusioned, he seeks the return of the contract he signed with the Devil. During his conversation Cipriano wrings from the Prince of Darkness a confession that he is powerless against the God of the Christians.

Fabio informs the governor of the capture of the Christians, Justina and Lisandro. The governor is overjoyed by the news and grants Fabio's request for the release of Lelio and Floro.

Cipriano declares that the God of the Christians is the one he now confesses; all else is "dust, smoke, ashes and wind." He eagerly awaits martyrdom in order to be redeemed. Justina speaks to him of God's great mercy and forgiveness. The governor orders their death by torture; thus the two are finally united in death.

In the midst of a violent storm the Devil appears before the governor, Lelio, Floro and others. He is forced by heaven to clear Justina's honor by revealing the truth, and admitting that he was the one who had entered Justina's apartment.

Plot Structure and Techniques—There are two plots—the main and the sub-plot. The religious or main action revolves around Cipriano's quest for a rational concept of the attributes of the true God. In his search he is confronted by two antagonists: the Devil who seeks to confound him by deliberate deception; and Justina who arouses his primitive passions that almost bring him to the brink of disaster.

The sub-plot is a romantic action which consists of two aspects: first, the efforts of two friends, Lelio and Floro, and ultimately Cipriano, to win the hand of Justina, a Christian. Second, the machinations of the Devil to bring about her downfall through temptation and the deliberate defamation of her character. The romantic plot is linked to the religious thematically through the discovery of truth. Cipriano's search for the true God and a concept of true love is equated with the disclosure of truth by the Devil and the subsequent removal of the stain to Justina's virtue.

The third action (it can hardly be labeled a plot) involving Clarín, Moscón and Livia is often a parody of a preceding serious action which it reinforces by means of contrast.

The main and secondary plots alternate and are built up by segments. Another feature of Calderón's technique in this play is to intermingle segments of the two actions in order to achieve a tighter unity. The three main characters, Cipriano, Justina and the Devil, figure in both plots. The Devil manipulates both actions: he causes confusion in the affairs of Cipriano, Justina and the suitors Floro and Lelio. Moreover, he deliberately hides the truth about God from Cipriano. Satan also sullies Justina's honor until a Higher Power forces him to divulge the truth.

Cipriano intervenes to halt a duel between Floro and Lelio, who are fighting over the affections of Justina, because his moral philosophy has taught him the difference between honor and infamy. He has developed a social consciousness that has made him aware of the latent dangers of ruining a woman's reputation when two or more suitors court her. His main purpose then in stopping the conflict is to prevent scandal. Cipriano offers to mediate the dispute by visiting her and asking her to select the one she loves. To reinforce this aspect of the plot, Calderón duplicates the idea in the third or reflector action. The clown Clarín informs the servant Livia of a similar motive for his visit, since Moscón also woos her.

The appearance of the Devil outside Justina's balcony paves the way for the subsequent denigration of her character. Muttering to himself, Satan reveals his intention of defaming her character. The confusion caused by the Devil's presence occasions another duel between Floro and Lelio. By his decision to abandon his studies and to devote himself to courting Justina, Cipriano, like

Floro and Lelio, will contribute to compounding the very scandal he seeks to avoid.

Justina rejects Lelio's advances lest she lose her good reputation. Lelio sees the figure of a man (Satan) on her balcony and believes the worst. As in so many *comedias,* the cause of the confusion and misunderstanding stems from the clash between appearance and reality. Floro refers to Justina's "hypocritical virtue," thinking that Lelio, whom he has spied hovering near the balcony, has free access to the house. When Floro and Lelio duel again, the governor, angered by the persistence of the feud, orders them both arrested. Ignorant of the whole truth (he sees only the "appearance"), he blames Justina. Lisandro, her guardian, also condemns her for what he saw.

The scene in which the Devil admits that it was God who protected Justina's reputation from scandal welds the romantic action to the religious. It causes Cipriano to reason that this God which kept her honor clean and pure is the Highest Goodness since it permitted no insult. Thus what started out as an abstraction, the definition of true God, becomes a living reality for Cipriano who observes that the God which protected Justina is Omniscient. When Cipriano announces his conversion to Christianity through the example of Justina, the governor orders her imprisoned for instigating a scandal in the city by her false virtue. Thus, like her mother, Justina suffers martyrdom because of deliberate deception, false appearances and incriminating circumstances.

The resolution takes the form of a deus ex machina in which the Devil is forced to admit his complete and sole guilt in defaming Justina's character. The romantic action then provides the means for demonstrating the practical application in everyday life of the principles of truth, justice and love developed in the religious action. Early in the play Cipriano through his reasoning arrives at a Christian concept of God. But his debate with the Devil turns out to be purely academic as he falls into the trap of the emotions from which he gradually extricates himself by means of a progressive revelation of truth accomplished through a disillusion, the power of reason, the help of Justina (who represents Divine Grace) and, ironically, the Devil's admissions and confessions. His experiences, largely amorous and passionate, are depicted in the romantic scenes in his confrontation with Justina from whom he learns that love is not promiscuity nor possessiveness but self-sacrifice. Moreover, in order to gain Justina's soul, the Devil attempts through deliberate falsehoods and circumstantial evidence to cast aspersions on her virtue. Cipriano's discovery of truth in regard to God and love is slow and gradual as is the denigration of Justina's reputation by the Devil which is in antithetical balance to it.

The governor, Lisandro, Floro and Lelio all discover the truth about Justina's virtue in the closing moments of the play when the Devil is forced to reveal it to them. Falsehood or deception, the opposite of truth, is employed by Satan to bring about the downfall of both Cipriano and Justina. He almost succeeds in the case of Cipriano who learns the truth for himself; in the case of Justina, she knows the truth and relies on God's help to sustain her. The romantic action which Menéndez y Pelayo considered an impediment to the main action is in reality an integral part of it, since it is on this plane of reality that the author chooses to clothe in dramatic form certain ideas he expounds on the religious plane.

Calderón injects many so-called cape-and-sword elements into the play: duels, jealousy, hidden lovers and the unexpected return of the girl's guardian which have led some critics to appraise the play adversely.[14] It must be remembered that the romantic plot is the practical application of the religious ideas imbedded in the main plot and that it was the dramatist's way of engaging the attention of his audience.

Another technique is Calderón's use of dialectics and casuistry. The great debate between Cipriano and the Devil in Act One is the principal example, though there are other instances of lesser importance in various parts of the play.

Dates of Composition, Publication and the Première—The play was probably written early in the year 1637. The autograph manuscript, which was formerly in the possession of the Duke of Osuna, is now in the Biblioteca Nacional of Madrid. It bears the date 1637 and the information that the work was composed for the village of Yepes in the province of Toledo on the occasion of the celebration of the Corpus Christi festival.

The play was not published until 1663 when it found its way into the large collection of *Escogidas* printed between the years

1652 and 1704. It appeared in *Parte veinte de comedias varias nunca impresas, compuestas por los mejores ingenios de España,* Madrid, 1663.

The French Hispanist, Alfred Morel-Fatio, was the first to utilize the manuscript in his edition of the play published in Heilbronn, 1877. Since the seventeenth century the play has appeared in about twenty-five single editions and numerous collections, which may give some hint of its popularity.

Sources and Treatment of Theme—Historical and Legendary. The basic source of the play is the martyrdom of two saints, Cyprian and Justina, who suffered death in 304 for devotion to the Christian God in the reign of the Roman Emperor Diocletian (284–315). Christians were also cruelly persecuted under an earlier Emperor, Decius (249–251) in whose reign one Cyprian, the Bishop of Carthage, suffered persecution and finally death in 258 in the reign of the Emperor Valerian (253–260).

Early writers of hagiographic history and others confused the two Cyprians. The historical fact is that the Cyprian of the play was not a bishop but a philosopher and magician living in Antioch. The subsequent treatment of these two Cyprians and the diffusion of the Cyprian-Justina legend has been studied in some detail by James Geddes in the Introduction to his edition of the play, *El mágico prodigioso,* New York: Holt, 1929, from which most of this information has been derived.

Calderón undoubtedly read about the martyrdom of Cyprian and Justina in the *Legenda aurea,* a collection of saints' lives written by the Italian Jacobus de Voragine (1230–1298). Geddes has found many verbal similarities between the *Legenda aurea* and the play and concludes that they were not merely fortuitous. However, there are discrepancies between the two, and Geddes has searched for other legendary sources from which Calderón could have derived his information. Another possible source was Alfonso de Villegas who had at his disposal a manuscript of the thirteenth or fourteenth century in the library of the cathedral of Toledo. By consulting also Gregory of Nazianzus and possibly Ortiz Lucio, Calderón was able thereby to enrich his subject matter.

Literary. Geddes discusses three plays by Calderón's contemporaries that also provided him with material for the play: two are by Mira de Amescua (1578–1640) and one by Guillén de Castro (1569–1631). The first is *The Devil's Slave* (*El esclavo del demonio*) with which *The Wonder-Working Magician* has so many points of resemblance that its influence on Calderón can hardly be denied. The second play by Mira is *The Gallant Hermit and the Heavenly Innkeeper's Wife* (*El ermitaño galán y la mesonera del cielo*).

The third play is *The Prodigy of the Mountains and Martyr of Heaven, Santa Barbara* (*El prodigio de los montes y mártir del cielo, Santa Bárbara*). Calderón has taken not only the ideas but also many expressions from this play by Castro. He worked over the material he extracted from these plays and produced a work that is far superior to its three immediate sources.

There have been many expressions of the Faust legend down the years. One of the first important manifestations in English literature is Christopher Marlowe's play, *Dr. Faustus* (1588). Goethe's *Faust,* which appeared in 1808, is the story of a sixteenth century necromancer and astrologer driven to sign a pact with the Devil in order to obtain knowledge, worldly goods and pleasures. Another phase of the legend in a different medium is the opera *Faust* (1859) by Gounod.

The English poet Percy B. Shelley became intensely interested in Calderón and translated several passages of *The Wonder-Working Magician* into English. The passages are quoted by Madariaga in his study of the two poets.[15] In a letter to John Gisborne, Shelley compares the Spanish and the German masterpieces:

> Have you read Calderón's *Mágico prodigioso?* I find a striking similarity between *Faust* and this drama, and if I were to acknowledge Coleridge's distinction, should say Goethe was the greatest philosopher and Calderón the greatest poet. Cyprian evidently furnished the germ of *Faust* as *Faust* may furnish the germ of other poems; although it is as different from it in structure and plan as the acorn is from the oak. I have—imagine my presumption—translated several scenes from both, as the basis of a paper for our journal. I am well content with those from Calderón, which in fact gave me very little trouble.

Shelley, like Calderón, approaches the problems of the world through the disciplines of poetry, metaphysics and theology. But Shelley relied on metaphysics whereas Calderón depended more on theology, which was the mainstay of his time. Calderón firmly believed in the Church and her teachings; in his theater he expresses his beliefs in various ways. Shelley in his doubt reveals his uneasiness with his position. Nevertheless, he admired the Spanish poet, perhaps because Calderón never faltered in his conviction that the Church alone possessed the truth about life and death.

In modern times Thomas Mann has essayed the Faust legend in his *Doktor Faustus* (1947).

Characterization—Cipriano. Although the leading character is drawn largely from the legend, Calderón has humanized him and endowed him with a nobility of spirit. He is a serious student of philosophy but falls a victim to Satan's snares since he has not been apprized of the stranger's true identity. Lacking a complete understanding of his natural desires, Cipriano yields to his concupiscible appetite. He studies magic not for purposes of self-aggrandizement but to conquer his lady-love. His conduct toward his friends exhibits nobleness of heart, and love of fair-play until he becomes their rival for the hand of Justina.

Justina. She is portrayed in the older versions of the legend as a feminine paragon of Christian idealism. Reared by a Christian foster father upon the death of her mother, Justina from early childhood has known about Christianity so that when she is importuned by suitors whom she does not love and by the Devil himself, through the use of her free will and by calling upon the name of God, she is able to withstand the onslaughts of the flesh. Even though her reputation is above reproach, nevertheless, because of the scandal raised by the dueling suitors, she becomes the object of the jealous suspicion on the part of the governor and even her foster father.

Lisandro is depicted as a sympathetic character because he has reared the young girl Justina at a great sacrifice to himself during the years of poverty and adversity. He has instructed her in the Christian faith which has become her bulwark against temptation. But Lisandro, like the governor, quickly judges the girl's reputation to have been sullied by the persistent, bickering suitors without finding out the truth of the affair for himself. The other characters are colorless and without interest except for one more figure in the play—the Devil.

The concept of the Devil as the head of a kingdom of demons with superhuman strength and knowledge probably comes from the Jews who in turn inherited the idea from an earlier people. Remarks about him in the Old and New Testaments provided the Church Fathers with a basic but incomplete image of the Prince of Darkness. Some imagined that Lucifer's expulsion from heaven was due to his pride, for he wished to occupy God's place. Others contended that Satan became dissatisfied after God created man in his own image. In order to avenge himself on God, he attempted to lead men astray and bring them to idolize him. He is partial to all forms of paganism and strives to win Christians to unbelief, sin and idolatrous practices since Christianity is his archenemy.

The Devil in the play assumes various disguises in order to hide his real identity and cover up his nefarious schemes. Since the disguises may take innocent-appearing forms like a traveler, for example, mankind finds itself in the dangerous position of being unable to recognize the Devil for what he is.

As the theater developed, the Devil found his way onto the stage beginning with the old mystery and morality plays of the Middle Ages. At first he was of an ugly and horrifying appearance —with a long red nose, cloven hoofs and a long tail. Later he wore red stockings and horns. Some devils were richly clothed in garments of gold and silver.

Professor Parker underlines a technique of Calderón's which must be taken into account if one is to understand the theme of the play more fully.[16] After the Devil, who comes disguised as a traveler, has informed Cipriano that he has lost his way to Antioch, the latter is amazed at such stupidity when the towers of the city are plainly visible before them. The Devil's answer is important: "That is what ignorance is: to be in sight of knowledge and not to know how to make use of it" (Esa es la ignorancia, / a la vista de las ciencias / no saber aprovecharlas.)

This is an example of willful ignorance due to a defect of attention by which one does not consider what should have been considered. This casual remark is a sign-post or guide to indicate the direction of the action: the Devil will try to prevent Cipriano from following through with his reasoning and thinking about the nature of God. Cipriano has already reached the point in his speculation that God must possess the attributes of "Unity, Goodness, Omniscience and Omnipotence." The final problem that remains to be solved is where can he find such a God? Hence the Devil appears at the psychological moment to prevent Cipriano from completing his search for truth, and to keep him in ignorance or in a state of emotional disturbance. The Devil, then, functions as a visual representation of what occurs in Cipriano's mind and emotions.

Interpretations—Professor Wardropper sees in the drama the interplay of wisdom and saintliness.[17] He considers the saint and the sage as the two ideal Christian types in the Church tradition: the saint's life was as near to Christ's in perfection as was humanly possible; the sage possessed the greatest degree of wisdom it was possible for humans to attain. Wisdom had to be differentiated from knowledge in that the former accepted divine revelation and the authority of the Church, made use of reason and adapted the results of knowledge to the problems of daily living.

Refusing to render homage to Jupiter whom his reason has shown to be a counterfeit deity, Cipriano has attained that natural perfection nearest to saintliness possible for a non-Christian. Moreover, he is of such a serious turn of mind as to eschew frivolities and to inspire confidence that his friends Lelio and Floro entrust the arbitration of their love dispute to him. Having studied Pliny and the essence and attributes of God, Cipriano the sage has reached the closest point possible to perfect wisdom for anyone not a Christian.

But since he has not yet attained Christian wisdom, he is easily susceptible to the power of the Devil. Satan first attacks Cipriano through the intellect and loses. His next move is an attack on the emotions. Cipriano's false concept of love as possession has caused him to interrupt his studies just when he was about to discover the true nature of God. Cipriano's fall is brought about by the imperfection of his wisdom and there occurs a series of intellectual, spiritual and emotional degradations.

When the Devil is unable to provide him with the body of Justina, Cipriano soon forces him to concede defeat by confessing that he is powerless before the Christian God who has protected Justina. By reason Cipriano is certain that the God who defended Justina can also save him. Calling upon the God of the Christians, Cipriano is at last able to overcome the power of Satan.

CHAPTER 8

The Historical Plays

THE historical plays are drawn largely from ancient times, and from the story of Spain down the centuries, especially in its wars with infidel and heretic; they are highly colored with a national consciousness of Catholic Spain, glorious and triumphant.[1] We shall now consider one of the most remarkable of the historical plays, *Daughter of the Air* (*La hija del aire*), Parts I and II; it offers an insight into the character of the too ambitious queen of Assyria, Semíramis.

I *Daughter of the Air* (*La hija del aire*)

The duo of plays known as *Daughter of the Air* is not merely a dramatization of a vaulting ambition but a vivid presentation of ambition's cause: an inordinate pride which finds in ambition one way to satisfy its egocentric nature. Else how explain the final sequence of Act Three, Part II, where Semíramis engages in a seemingly unnecessary battle with a rival who is withdrawing? Here ambition turns to personal revenge to compensate for the insecurity and inadequacy she has experienced as a wife, queen and mother.

Calderón may have found the material for the play in the histories of Diodorus, Strabo and Herodotus, or his more immediate source may have been the first three-act play by Cristóbal de Virués, *La gran Semíramis.*

The character of Semíramis has captivated the minds of men down the centuries and has found expression in art, music and literature. In France, Crébillon and Voltaire wrote of Semíramis in 1717 and 1743 respectively. An opera by Gluck was completed in 1748, and Rossini's overture, *Semiramide,* in 1823. There is an unfinished picture by Degas, and Paul Valéry was one of the most recent writers to essay the story.

Plot Summary—Part One. Semíramis, whose mother had perished in childbirth, has been brought up by an old priest, Tiresias. Menón, a general in the Assyrian army of King Nino, returns victorious from the wars. Menón falls in love with Nino's sister, Irene.

During a trek through the jungle, Menón comes upon Semíramis, who has been held captive by Tiresias in a cave. Menón, apparently forgetting Irene, falls in love with Semíramis and frees her from her imprisonment. He brings her to his country estate where he asks her to remain.

Back in the palace of Nineveh, Menón, by his description of Semíramis' beauty, arouses Nino's desire to see her. Semíramis falls in love with Nino, but she cannot reveal her identity to him. Grateful to Menón for liberating her, Semíramis envisages a marriage with him. Nino threatens to gouge out Menón's eyes if he dares look upon Semíramis.

Motivated by jealousy, Irene urges Semíramis to pretend to Nino that she has lost interest in Menón. Also driven by jealousy, Nino orders Menón to inform Semíramis that his love for her has waned. He also warns his general (Menón) that if he goes through with the wedding, he will be stripped of all honor and favor. Semíramis finally accepts Nino as a husband, hopeful of seizing power after she becomes queen. She forbids Nino to deprive Menón of life and liberty. Nino complies with her request, but in his anger, he orders Menón's eyes gouged out.

Part Two. Between the two parts, Nino has died and Semíramis occupies the throne. Lidoro, King of Lidia, appears as his own ambassador, to plead his claim to the Assyrian throne. Lidoro had married Nino's sister, Irene, who bore him a son, Irán. Furthermore, there is the popular rumor that Semíramis poisoned her husband in her haste to seize complete power for herself. Semíramis argues that she had no reason to kill her husband as she already controlled the reins of government. Moreover, her son Ninias is of so effeminate a nature that she considers him incapable of ruling. A battle ensues and Semíramis captures Lidoro, who now despairs of the rule of reason. The two brothers Licas and Friso, advisers of the Queen, are divided over the treatment of the prisoner: Licas favors mercy, Friso demands punishment.

An unexpected reversal of fortune occurs when the people rebel in favor of Ninias. Vowing revenge on the populace, Semíramis abdicates, but only temporarily, withdrawing to the innermost recesses of the palace. On his way to express his gratitude to his mother, Ninias comes upon Lidoro and, having pity on him, promises him freedom. But an old and wise counselor, Lisías, advises Ninias to keep Lidoro under protective custody.

Semíramis and Friso unite their forces and kidnap Ninias. Because of the likeness in physical appearance between mother and son, the Queen masquerades as Ninias without anyone's suspecting her real identity. Semíramis punishes Lidoro for his support of Ninias and Nino and his opposition to her.

The confusion in the political action caused by Semíramis' impersonation of Ninias is also mirrored in the romantic action. Experiencing pangs of jealousy, Licas surmises that Ninias (Semíramis) is in love with Libia, his sweetheart. Astrea, daughter of Lisías, is also baffled by Ninias' (Semíramis') change of heart.

Lidoro escapes from the prison tower. The opposing armies of Lidoro and Semíramis clash and the Queen is wounded. In a fleeting but impressive flash of hallucination before her death, Semíramis feels pangs of a guilty conscience as the figures of Menón, Nino and Ninias pass before her like souls in purgatory.

Plot Structure and Techniques—The single plot of Part I is split into two romantic aspects. Menón's description of Semíramis' beauty functions as a catalytic agent, touching off two actions: first, it occasions jealousy in Irene and entangles her, Menón and Semíramis in a web of love; second, it stimulates Nino's desire to meet the "rational beast" and fashions another triangular love affair involving Menón, Semíramis and Nino.

A political plot, which will be more fully developed in the second part, appears only in fragmentary form in the third act of Part I. The seeds of its later development, however, are sown early in Act One from Venus' prophecy as it was given to Tiresias. It stated that Semíramis would be the terror of the world, instigating tragedy, death, insult, wrath, weeping and confusion. And also that her love would convert a King (Nino) into a tyrant whom she would then proceed to kill.

Flashback and Prophecy. Semíramis' narration of the circumstances of her birth, early in Part I, provides the reader with background information in order that he may better understand her situation. Her mother, Arceta, had slain her seducer and had died during childbirth. Semíramis was found by an old priest, Tiresias, who, learning of the prognostication of her fate from his study of astrology, later imprisoned her in a cave. Before that, Diana, ashamed that one of her nymphs (Semíramis' mother) had been violated, wanted to hide her (Semíramis) in the belly of a beast, but Venus sent the birds to bring her nourishment and defend her. Hence her name Semíramis, which in Assyrian means "bird" (and hence the title, *Daughter of the Air*). Mindful of the prophecy, Semíramis is confident that she can conquer her fate since heaven never forces the will.

Calderón here, as elsewhere in his theater, associates the two ideas of freedom and free will together. After Menón has released Semíramis from her prison-like environment, he requests that she remain in his country estate while he is away on business. He is careful to emphasize that her sojourn there is not an imprisonment, but rather a preventive measure against an adverse fate. After he leaves, she debates with herself whether or not she has free will, having been transferred from one prison to another.

Conflict. Two types of conflict develop in the First Part: exterior and interior. The exterior conflict between Nino and Menón revolves around their love for Semíramis. The interior conflict takes place in the minds of Nino and Irene and is expressed partly in the asides. It involves a clash between appearance and reality. Both Nino and Irene must look after their own interests. Hence they say one thing to Semíramis and Menón, but in reality their true feelings are hidden in the asides. Nino hopes he can postpone the wedding of Menón and Semíramis. Motivated by jealousy (she is furious at Menón for deserting her in favor of Semíramis), Irene approves of her brother's idea to delay the wedding.

The dramatic function of Irene becomes more apparent in Act Three when she creates a false reality for Semíramis which will conclude in a true reality. Motivated by jealousy, Irene orders

Semíramis to pretend to Nino that she is no longer interested in marrying Menón. This false reality or "appearance" will touch off a chain reaction: it will encourage the King in his love affair with Semíramis, and at the same time it will mirror a false reality which Nino will create for Menón. Furthermore, Irene wants Semíramis to give Menón to understand that she hates him. To insure the success of her plan, Irene hides in ambush to overhear the conversation.

An immediate parallel is set up when Nino orders Menón to indicate to Semíramis that his ardor for her has cooled. Likewise, Nino hides in order to eavesdrop on the dialogue. Nino's motivation is also jealousy. Both Semíramis and Menón are plunged into a dilemma: how can they pretend hatred for the ones they love? Throughout this scene their true feelings are expressed in asides.

The complexity of the situation is increased by the addition of another level of reality involving the eyes and ears of Semíramis and Menón. In an aside to her, Menón urges her to disregard what she hears and to watch only his eyes. However, before this device can be used, there is an intensification of the theme of hatred. Both Irene and Nino demand a stronger statement of the mutual hate between Semíramis and Menón. In stichomythic dialogue, Semíramis and Menón recognize their mutual suffering and cross over to the opposite ends of the stage; Menón finds Irene and Semíramis finds Nino. This cross-over represents the reversal, or change, that was not evident at the opening of this sequence, but that now becomes the only reality.

The structure of Part Two rests on two actions; one political, the other romantic. The political plot concerns Semíramis' plans to crush her enemies and to usurp the throne from her son Ninias. The romantic plot revolves around a triangle wherein both Ninias and Friso are in love with Astrea. Semíramis loves Licas; the latter does not reciprocate her love since he has given his hand to Libia. The two plots are linked by the theme of infidelity and treason and the action stems once again from the incongruity between reality and appearance.

After Semíramis has abdicated in favor of her son, she vows vengeance on the populace who has forced her to resign. Her abdication is only the semblance of reality; the inner reality is her longing to rule. In an aside she rages, "I without a command! I am raging with anger! I without a kingdom! I'm losing my mind. I have become a raging Mount Etna, I spew forth flames; I am a volcano, I breathe thunderbolts."

Appearance versus Reality. After Semíramis has donned the attire of her son, Licas and Lisías are amazed at the apparent change in the monarch, a change they find difficult to reconcile with "his" former effeminate character. In addition to creating confusion in the political sphere, Semíramis' assumption of Ninias' identity produces chaos also in the romantic action. Thinking that he is talking to Ninias, Licas experiences pangs of jealousy because he presumes that Ninias is in love with Libia. Likewise, Astrea accuses Ninias (Semíramis) of changing his mind in matters of the heart. Hence the love affair terminates in utter confusion. Licas reproaches Libia for stating that the King (Ninias) loves her, and Friso reproves Astrea for the same reason. The idea of infidelity enters the minds of the lovers and mirrors the theme of treason in the political action.

Characterization—The *de casibus* tragedies, which flooded western Europe during the Renaissance, usually treated historical subjects because of their verisimilitude, since it was reasoned that an audience would be acquainted with the well-known stories of fallen rulers.[2] No attempt was made to portray the protagonist as midway between good and bad; rather, he was entirely bad, a dangerous villain, ruthless, and wielding tyrannical powers.

Such a character is Semíramis, who excites admiration for her unbridled imagination, lust for power, nefarious schemes, recklessness and villainy. Semíramis, like Lady Macbeth, is the personification of evil. Her worldly greatness is treated by Calderón as both a fascination and a fatality. The notion of tragedy as a fall from greatness lent itself especially well to the treatment of ambition and its consequences. To yield to pride and to strive for power exposes one to the risks of temptation and the caprice of Fortune. Semíramis cannot subject her furious passion to the rule of reason. Like a beast, she must sate it completely before she can desist. She is pitiable only in the very helplessness to which she is driven by her passion.

Like Echo in Calderón's *Echo and Narcissus* (*Eco y Narciso*),

Queen Semíramis is incapable of love, using it only as a stepping stone to power, and so perishes. But even greater than her ambition and her lust for power is her pride. Once the egocentric Semíramis has gained position and power, she is still discontented. This inflated pride is the basic fault in her character that proves her undoing.

In her cruelty she treats Lidoro literally as a dog, humiliating him by feeding him dog food and placing him on a leash because he is her rival for the throne of Assyria. Then her vanity asserts itself as she temporarily lays aside the weapons of war to pretty herself. She combs her hair and finishes her make-up.

In defense of her "right" to rule, Semíramis claims lineage with the gods to enlarge her noble, goddess-like figure endowed with great power. In the characterization of Semíramis, Calderón points up an interplay between the two sides of her nature, the light and the dark. When the dark aspect is stressed, Semíramis is like the sirens of old, possessing the power to lure men to their destruction. This type appears time and again in myth and literature as goddess, nymph and mermaid.

An example of the "light" side of her character appears in her compassion for Menón in Part I because he "liberated" her from captivity.

In Part II, after Semíramis has kidnapped her son, she dons his clothing and rules in his place. Like the snake which sheds its skin, Semíramis has cast off every vestige of her former self. What was once concealed by the dress of femininity has now been torn asunder and exposes the "mannish woman" in all the stark reality of her evil nature. In this remarkable scene and in others to follow, every shred of what was decent has been flung to the winds; her former pity, gratitude and concern for the dignity of man have all disappeared.

Act Three of the Second Part touches upon Semíramis' cruelty, her almost complete indifference to the cause of justice, her disregard for the tempered advice of Lisías, her vindictiveness, her lust for power, and her unrestrained joy over the opportunity to "prove herself" in battle.

The Queen derives complete satisfaction from seeing herself idolized now by the very ones who formerly despised her. The applause of the populace inflates her ego. One by one she will deal in her own way with those who supported Ninias. Her decisions will be cruel, spiteful and unjust. She metes out the punishment of imprisonment to Chato for asking for a payment due him. She hangs a soldier for sedition. She deals harshly with Lidoro who sought the throne, pointing out to him "your ambition made you look for false propositions."

Toward the end of the play, Semíramis, in an outburst of rage, challenges Lidoro's armies. During the course of the battle she falls mortally wounded. Steadfastly denying her guilt, Semíramis gives up her life with these words, "I was a daughter of the air, now I shall vanish into it."

Ninias is depicted as effeminate and cowardly by those around him. However, he is not easily swayed by the acclaim of the people. He is aware of his obligations. He renders homage to his deceased father to whom he expresses his gratitude.

Ninias recognizes his own shortcomings, especially his haste in reaching important decisions without due reflection. He appoints Lisías as a judge because the latter acts as a brake on the lad's youthful and impetuous decisions.

Ninias shows himself to be compassionate, grateful, liberal and magnanimous. He keeps his word to Lidoro to whom he grants complete freedom.

Friso is portrayed as a shrewd opportunist, cognizant that Semíramis' decision to abdicate was made in haste, in anger and without prudence. He is selfish and envious. Blinded by passion and rage, he refuses Licas' offer to share his good fortune in being named commander of all forces on land and sea by Ninias. During the course of the play he becomes boastful, discontented, vindictive and treacherous, quick to anger and slow to forget an affront.

Symbolism and Imagery—As the play opens we find Semíramis dressed in skins which represent her animal-like nature. The human-animal dichotomy mirrors the ambivalent emotions of hate and love which she experiences upon the return of King Nino. The cave in which she has been brought up symbolizes her separation from society and her forthcoming inability to adjust to a normal environment.

The cave may also represent death for Semíramis, and Calderón expresses it in the imagery of "corpse," "entombed," and "tomb." The cave not only restricts her freedom of movement to its narrow confines; it also shackles her will and impedes her self-development. In time she becomes aware of the unauspicious augury, but she remains undaunted; she prefers to be killed by *truth* rather than by her *imagination.* Semíramis believes that he who dies because of fear is twice a coward. She has imagined what life must be like outside the cave; now that her endurance has reached the breaking point and her ambition is unrestrained, she wants to discover for herself the *truth* about life. Because of her lack of education and her maladjusted personality, she will be totally unprepared to cope with the problems of her environment. She inhabits the "confused labyrinth of thickly tangled underbrush and ill-formed rocks," a suitable milieu for the "monster of fortune" imprisoned in the wild, untamed country.

Menón's description of Semíramis in Part I, Act One, is important because it unites the imagery of her excessive passion for governing with the prognostication made by Venus.[3] The description begins with her hair, which is divided into two long tresses falling over her neck. The stress on the unruliness of her hair is meant to emphasize her own surly character. Next, he describes her forehead: "the hair usurped the domination of the brow;" this presages her later usurpation of power.

Irene's jealousy over Menón's description of Semíramis' beauty is all-consuming. She demands that he hand over the key to her garden. The key in this episode may be taken as a sexual symbol, and its return to Irene at this point signifies that she has terminated her amorous relationship with Menón.

Friso comes at night to a garden, induced by the note from an "afflicted woman" whose identity he does not yet know. Gripped by fear of the unknown, he addresses himself to the night, "goddess of sleep and forgetfulness," to whose "jet black deity" he will construct a temple of "black sorrowful jasper." The imagery of blackness, obscurity and darkness evokes an atmosphere of evil and foreboding which prepares the reader for the diabolical scheme of Semíramis soon to be disclosed. Suddenly the Queen appears, garbed in mourning because she has neither honor, being, nor life. Since her pride has been wounded by Ninias' scorn, Friso grasps at any opportunity for revenge. Semíramis has concocted a plan to kidnap her son, don his clothes and rule in his place. But she needs Friso's aid; alone she feels insufficient to the undertaking. The protective cover of night will conceal her crime. Her black robe like a nocturnal cloak hides her real motives. Her uncontrollable desire for power is the motivating force, pushing her to govern: "my kingdom is my life; since I am not its ruler, I am dead."

CHAPTER 9

The Honor Tragedies

THE four plays usually classified as "honor" tragedies are *For a Secret Insult, a Secret Vengeance* (*A secreto agravio, secreta venganza*),[1] *The Painter of His Dishonor* (*El pintor de su deshonra*), *The Physician of His Honor* (*El médico de su honra*), and *Jealousy, the Greatest Monster* (*El mayor monstruo los celos*). All deal tragically with the moving theme of honor in which a guiltless person perishes (in all but one, *The Painter of His Dishonor*) because of the breath of scandal, egoism and a frenzied imagination which invents the circumstances of guilt. The plays we have selected for study are *Jealousy, the Greatest Monster*[2] and *The Physician of His Honor*. The former is a stirring tragedy whose impact is expressed in terms of great lyric beauty, deep emotional conflict and heart-rending situations.

I *Jealousy, The Greatest Monster* (*El mayor monstruo los celos*)

Plot Summary—Mariana, wife of the Tetrarch Herodes, is sad over the prophecy that her husband's dagger will slay her. In his mad desire to make Mariana queen of the world so she will not have to envy anyone, Herodes has sent assistance to Marco Antonio in his campaign against Octaviano, the Emperor.

Octaviano has defeated the armada sent by Herodes and captured Mariana's brother, Aristóbolo. A box containing a letter revealing Herodes' treachery and a picture of Mariana falls into the Emperor's hands. The picture ignites Octaviano's passion for the unknown woman.

Tolomeo, a soldier who has just returned from the battle, informs Herodes of the defeat of his forces. In a vain attempt to assuage Mariana's sadness, the Tetrarch places his dagger at her feet and tells her again of his deep love for her.

Octaviano triumphantly enters the city of Jerusalem, receiving the plaudits of the crowd. When Herodes spies a picture of Mariana in the Emperor's hand, he suspects him of deception and attempts in vain to have him killed. The Tetrarch's inordinate jealousy reaches such intensity that he entrusts the mission of killing his wife to Filipo and Tolomeo, in the event he dies first.

The letter revealing Herodes' treachery falls into Mariana's hands, and she becomes more and more alarmed at the turn of events. She succeeds in getting Octaviano to pardon Herodes for his treachery. She then upbraids her husband for his cold-blooded letter. This angers Herodes, who tries to slay Tolomeo because he concludes that the soldier has revealed his plan to Mariana.

In a quarrel over her picture, Mariana escapes from Octaviano when she recognizes her husband's dagger in the Emperor's possession. In the ensuing struggle some of her garments are left on the floor. When Herodes sees the circumstantial evidence, he suspects her of infidelity. But a moment later, when he finds her fleeing the Emperor, the Tetrarch rushes to her defense. In the darkness he kills Mariana as the prophecy predicted, but by mistake. On discovering his error, he leaps out the window to his death.

The Play as Tragedy—The "new" tragedy that seventeenth century Spanish playwrights were essaying came from their interpretation of Aristotle's concept of *admiratio.* By it they meant surprise or astonishment over the outcome of an action. The incidents which arouse pity and fear sometimes take an unexpected turn and result in what modern critics call tragic irony. In the play Herodes realizes at the last moment that his wife is innocent of the infidelity he has suspected, and so he hastens to defend her against the persistent Octaviano. By a strange quirk of fate he kills Mariana in the darkness, mistaking her for the Emperor. For this costly error, he takes his own life. There is in the dénouement a double shock—the shock of recognition of an error by Herodes and the shock experienced by the audience when it witnessed the death of an innocent victim.

González de Sales, a Spanish dramatic theorist of the seventeenth century, and a follower of Aristotle, justified this type of ending with an unusual twist on the grounds that it produced a third emotion which he termed "disturbance" or "upset," or "confusion" (in Spanish the terms used are *turbación* and *perturbación*), and which he considered as appropriate to tragedy as pity or fear.

While Calderón has not left any theoretical statement on drama comparable to Lope's in the *New Art of Playwriting* (*Arte nuevo de hacer comedias*), discussed in Chapter One,[3] he defines tragedy briefly as "the decline of happiness." He was probably familiar with late sixteenth-century tragedies, including the versions of Herodes and Mariana (discussed in note 2) as well as the familiar story of Marc Anthony and Cleopatra which had already been the subject of a tragic drama by Shakespeare.

Apart from the "surprise" ending, Calderón's conception of tragedy, as revealed in the play, follows that of Lope and the Italian interpreters of Aristotle in the Renaissance. The leading characters are kings, princes, or great captains. The theme is taken from history and deals with deeds of blood and violence. The elevated and sublime style of tragedy is maintained. The characters never change from their original motives—this means that their end has to be tragic. In order to reach a tragic dimension, the passions and emotions of the characters are intense and exaggerated. Their despair and anxiety are tragically accentuated by moments of supreme hope. An ardent spirituality is constantly contrasted with an earthy, passionate sensuality. The exaggerated formalism, and the striving for subtle and florid ornamentation accompany a virulent realism and erotic intensity. Herodes is possessed of an ardent desire to attain the impossible. He is endowed with a weakness which brings about his ultimate downfall and the death of the one he loves most. To a large extent the author of his own woes, the Tetrarch, who regards himself as the personification of human misery and suffering, creates the mental and emotional stresses which provide the deeper tragedy of the play.

The purgative character of Herodes' examination of conscience serves as an Aristotelian catharsis, but in this case it is to purge the passions. The remarks made by various characters in the play on the action resemble the comments of the Greek chorus, so essentially a part of classical tragedy; the decline of happiness for all the leading characters, and the constant foreboding of impending disaster accentuate the tragic mode of the play. The dazzling display of imagery and rhetorical figures to depict the preoccupation with death, the love-madness, infatuation and ambition, the struggle for power, the treason, the vanity of this world, all coincide harmoniously with the underlying tragic tone of the work.

Plot Structure and Technical Devices—The main plot is romantic in nature. It consists of a love triangle created out of the imagination and machination of Herodes. He loves his wife so ardently that he will stop at nothing, even treason and murder, to cater to her every fancy, even to making her queen of the ancient world. To do this he must first defeat the Emperor Octaviano. Imbedded in the main romantic action is the political action revolving around Herodes' abortive attempt to usurp the power of the Emperor. When he sees a picture of Mariana in Octaviano's possession, he suspects his wife of infidelity. In reality, the picture has fallen into the Emperor's hands by chance. The creation of a pseudo-love triangle serves to unite the two actions. They are also linked by the themes of infidelity and treason. There is also a secondary romantic action involving Sirene, Tolomeo and Libia. It is a dim reflector triangle of the principal romantic action.

Calderón fashions each action separately and by segments. The two actions, romantic and political, evolve alternately. The protagonist, Herodes, is not confronted with the antagonist, Octaviano, until Act Two when the dramatist begins to blend the two actions into an inseparable whole. The two actions are still more tightly joined in Act Three when Octaviano meets Mariana. The secondary romantic action is phased out toward the end of Act Two.

The dénouement has been criticized as weak since Mariana is killed by mistake. The prophecy that Herodes would kill the one he loves most is fulfilled, but not in the way the reader expected. Should one, perhaps, suspect that Mariana's death (by mistake) is Calderón's way of providing the novel twist designed to arouse feelings of surprise and astonishment in the reader? One recognizes that it points up the role of the dagger which represents fate in the play.

The play is a coalescence of traditional dramatic devices, principally Senecan and Aristotelian. There is abundant balance and contrast not only in the plot structure, but also in the linguistic style which underscores the dramatic conflicts. The evidence of cause and effect in the arrangement of the episodes indicates that the play had been conceived with the utmost care. It is full of the theatrical and the sensational to intensify its impact on the reader and audience. Its conceptual adornments, of which Calderón was so fond, place in relief the poetic depiction of jealousy. Because of an undisciplined imagination, the Tetrarch creates another reality which differs from the dramatic reality in that the former exists only in his mind. He forges this pseudo-reality not only for himself, but also for Mariana and Octaviano as well as for some of the minor characters. We shall now examine more closely some of the so-called Senecan devices.

The representation of Herodes as a raging tyrant, with emphasis on the interior reality of the disturbed conscience, follows Senecan tradition. His uncontrollable fury is expressed in long-winded speeches often called fanfaronnade. His bluster permeates the entire dramatic fabric; at times it reaches the heights of magniloquence. The soliloquy is the vehicle par excellence for the expressions of his bravado.

The dagger, mentioned in the prophecy as the instrument of Mariana's death, works almost incredible wonders. It is tossed out a window by Herodes and wounds Tolomeo. In Act Two it symbolically pierces Mariana's picture which has just fallen from above the doorway through which Octaviano has passed. Thus Herodes' attempt to slay the Emperor in a burst of jealous rage is thwarted. The piercing of the picture foreshadows symbolically what will happen in the dénouement when Herodes inadvertently slays his wife, mistaking her in the darkness and confusion for Octaviano.

Mariana is profoundly moved by an astrologer's prophecy that she will die by her husband's dagger. This prediction occasions a sadness in the Queen that cannot be assuaged. Her deep melancholy arouses in the Tetrarch's warped mind a feeling of jealousy and anxiety. His jealousy, which is only a figment of his imagination, underscores the mental instability of the protagonist—a tragic flaw which will in time overturn his reason, and cause his fall, the death of his wife, and his own suicide. Even though Mariana rejects Octaviano's advances, the Tetrarch is so convinced of a liaison that it will prove his undoing. This situation represents the appearance versus fact type of conflict which Calderón often employs to produce dramatic tension.

Toward the end of Act One the Tetrarch, with egotistical bravado, refuses to take his wife's advice and flee before the advancing armies of the Emperor. The real reversal of Herodes on the military level, the defeat of his naval forces sent to aid Anthony and Cleopatra, and his capture by Octaviano, contrasts with his earlier apparent reversal in which his jealousy had blinded him into thinking he had lost his wife's affection and fidelity.

The idea of infidelity in the main action is mirrored in an episode of the secondary action. After Filipo delivers Herodes' letter to Tolomeo, he reveals his true character by suggesting that the secret order be ignored for, if the Tetrarch dies, who is to obey a dead man? Sirene, a lady-in-waiting to Mariana, becomes jealous when she mistakes the letter for a billet-doux from Libia, her rival for the hand of Tolomeo. As in the principal action, the charge of infidelity is groundless and is spawned of circumstantial and misleading evidence.

Character Depiction—Herodes is consumed by an overpowering love for his wife that passes beyond what most people would regard as normal. His love is so intense that it blinds him to everything moral and rational. It leads him to treason and an attempted murder in order to accomplish what he thinks will make Mariana happy, viz., that, being Queen of the Roman Empire, she will have nobody to envy. Calderón states that "when love is not madness, it is not love." This idea, of course, was not new, as many writers of ancient times considered love a madness.[4]

From his great love comes a jealousy so passionate that Herodes cannot bear anyone's possessing Mariana except himself. This deep-seated jealousy drives him to stipulate that in the event he dies first, Filipo and Tolomeo are to slay Mariana. Herodes' jealousy is the greatest monster in the world and is the cause of his downfall.[5] It derives from an unbridled imagination that leads the Tetrarch to accept circumstantial evidence as proof positive of his wife's infidelity.

Herodes' frenzy breaks out in all its fury when he attempts to slay Tolomeo, thinking that the latter has betrayed his secret to

Mariana. Herodes' warped and twisted mind is not interested in ascertaining the truth in this situation or in any other that concerns his wife. Calderón follows the traditional concept of depicting Herodes as a raging tyrant that gave rise to our expression "to out-Herod Herod."

The portrayal of all the other characters is subordinated to that of Herodes. Mariana loves her husband and suffers from extreme melancholia after learning of the terrible prophecy. However, once she is stirred to action, she is not afraid to reproach her husband for his nefarious scheme. She remains faithful to Herodes and never encourages the amorous advances of the Emperor.

Octaviano falls a victim to Mariana's beauty and succumbs to her pleas. In his magnanimity, or in deference to her wishes, he not only pardons Herodes for his treachery but also restores him to his former position and honor.

II *The Physician of His Honor* (*El médico de su honra*)

Act One. Near the outskirts of Seville, Prince Enrique falls from his horse during a hunting expedition. His two courtiers Arias and Diego are surprised by the action of King Pedro who abandons his injured brother in order to enter the city. From the tower of her country house, Doña Mencía has witnessed the entire incident. Her servant Jacinta announces that they are bringing the injured Prince to her house. Since Mencía once loved Enrique, she fears for her honor.

When Enrique regains consciousness, Mencía informs him that she is now married. Her husband Gutierre appears and Enrique in veiled language tells him the story of a woman who, although engaged to one man, married another. Gutierre agrees it was wrong, but Mencía advises him to hear the woman's side of the incident.

After Enrique has left, Gutierre decides to enter Seville to pay his respects to the King. Mencía becomes jealous, thinking that Gutierre is going to visit his former girl friend, Leonor. After Gutierre leaves, Mencía confides to her servant Jacinta that Enrique once loved her. She disdained him and her father married her off to Gutierre.

In Seville, Leonor appears masked to air her grievances to the King. She was once engaged to Gutierre, but he deserted her. Later Gutierre explains to the monarch that he found another man in Leonor's house. The unknown man is later identified as Don Arias who maintains he was not in search of Leonor but of another woman. The King imprisons Gutierre and Arias for threatening a duel.

Act Two. Enrique gains admittance to Mencía's garden by bribing the servant and slave Jacinta with a promise of liberty. He gazes upon the sleeping Mencía whom he still loves.

In the meantime, Gutierre has secured permission from the warden to return home to visit his wife. Mencía quickly hides Enrique in her room. After greeting Gutierre, she leaves to prepare his supper. She re-enters hurriedly with the news that there is a strange man in the house. The lights are extinguished, and in the confusion Jacinta dismisses Enrique.

Gutierre finds a dagger and suspects something is afoot. When Mencía spies the dagger in her husband's possession, she fears for her life.

Back at the court, the King has Gutierre and Arias pledge friendship. Gutierre discovers that the dagger belongs to Enrique. Being the physician of his own honor, Gutierre prescribes silence and patience for himself. He plans to return home secretly that night to carry out a nefarious scheme. In the meantime, Leonor rejects Arias since she still loves Gutierre.

Jumping over the wall, Gutierre finds his wife asleep in the garden. When she awakens, she cannot discern the identity of the intruder in the darkness and addresses him as "your Highness." Gutierre's suspicions of his wife's infidelity are confirmed. She hides him as Jacinta approaches with a light. Gutierre then re-enters and presents himself as if nothing has happened, having gained admittance by using his own key.

Act Three. Gutierre informs the King that he believes Enrique was in his house since he found the dagger there. The Prince claims he does not remember where he lost the weapon. As the King offers it to him, Enrique accidentally cuts the monarch's hand. The King believes the Prince has deceived him and Enrique decides to leave Seville. Gutierre, who has overheard the conversation, considers his wife guilty and secretly plans to kill her.

Mencía confides to Jacinta that she is terribly confused about the identity of the man she spoke to last night. When news arrives of Enrique's falling out with his brother and his imminent departure, Jacinta advises Mencía to write and request that he not leave as such an act might incriminate her.

After Gutierre enters, he reads his wife's letter and is more convinced than ever of her infidelity. Dismissing the servants and locking Mancía in her room, he writes her a note, warning her that she has only two more hours of life in which to prepare herself for death.

Gutierre commissions Ludovico, a bloodletter, to bleed Mencía to death or be killed. Later that same evening, the King and Diego spot two men coming down the street—Gutierre and Ludovico. The former flees and Ludovico tells how he was forced to bleed an innocent woman to death. He had sufficient presence of mind to leave his bloody finger marks on the house walls.

Gutierre emerges from his house just as the King arrives. He pretends to be grief-stricken because a bloodletter permitted Mencía to bleed to death. The King accepts the explanation and suggests that Gutierre marry Leonor. The latter evinces no surprise or fear of a hand bathed in blood; in fact, she expects the same treatment if she is suspected of infidelity.

The Poetic Approach to the Play—Professor Bruce W. Wardropper, in a penetrating study of the play, suggests that it should be considered primarily as poetry rather than as drama.[6] Poetry, following a long tradition of dramatic verse, calls upon drama in its various aspects of characterization, plot and dialogue to serve it. He feels that one should study any given aspect of the poetry of the play—in this case, the images—in much the same way as one studies lyric poetry.

The entire play should be viewed as a full-blown metaphor in which Gutierre is the physician of his honor only in a figurative sense. Mencía is to be considered as the patient (honor) and the malady is dishonor. After making a diagnosis, the physician prescribes a remedy—bleeding; not to cure the *patient* but the *malady*. In other words the *human* element in the problem, the patient, is the least important; the honor of the man whose reputation may be damaged is all-important. This startling concept, according to Wardropper, follows the esthetic doctrine of *admiratio* (wonderment) and is part of the new concept of catharsis, a fusion of Aristotelian terror and pity and expounded by Alonso López Pinciano in his *Ancient Poetic Philosophy* (*Filosofía poética antigua*).

To make the metaphor more plausible, Calderón selects those images which are drawn from more realistic sources. Mencía's metaphorical fall from honor is anticipated at the opening of the play by Enrique's literal fall from his horse. Moreover, Enrique is the cause of Mencía's honor problems.

Wardropper states that the honor play is the typical tragedy of the Spanish baroque period since it always involves married couples, whereas baroque comedy treats the theme of love lightly and is always enacted by unmarried couples.

The tragic web of circumstances has already engulfed Gutierre before the play opens since he had previously dishonored Leonor. She secretly prays for revenge and in time she gets what she wants—the hand of Gutierre after the latter has had his wife slain. One gets the impression that mysterious forces moved by the hand of God have intervened in the action of the play. Mencía is removed as an obstacle to the marriage of Gutierre and Leonor as if she were a pawn on the chess board of life, a tragic victim of Fate.

According to Wardropper, there are three series of images that mirror the fateful events. The first group may be classified as mythological and astral. The former are called into play in order to describe a beautiful woman and the latter to exalt royalty. They reflect a kind of divine perfection. In contrast, man's imperfection is described by metaphors of restraint and containment: usually doors and prisons. The third group consists of images founded on the cosmos, i.e., meteorology and the four elements of which the universe was thought to be composed. These images also derive reinforcement from nature: "blood, rose; mountain, jealousy; basilisk, love; weeds, dishonor; light, life; and night, death." The symbol of light is so important to the author that he repeats it often—the extinction of light either conceals or suggests dishonor.

Professor Wardropper concludes that *The Physician of His Honor* is "a moving tragedy, explicable in terms of the play itself and organized around a body of poetic imagery which, though not logical in the logician's sense of the word, contains its own rationale."

The Plot Structure—The plot of the play follows a linear progression, a single action thrown into relief by parallelism, by contrast, and by variations on the theme of honor. It concerns the efforts of Don Gutierre to remove the apparent stain on his honor. His problem is that he cannot kill the one he believes to be the offender, since the latter is of royal blood. Therefore he must slay the other presumably guilty party, his own wife, Doña Mencía. Gutierre had first loved Doña Leonor, but on finding a man (Don Arias) in her apartment, he had broken his promise to her. A dim reflector action is Leonor's striving to regain her lost honor by appealing to the King to compel Gutierre to marry her. Since Gutierre is already married, the King is unable to comply with the request. Doña Mencía's marriage to Gutierre had been arranged by her father when she could not marry Prince Enrique, whom she really loved, because he was away on military duty. However, now that she is married, she cannot allow her honor to be tarnished by the advances of the Prince. Nor can the King allow his brother Enrique to becloud the royal honor by paying court to a married woman. Finally, because there is enmity between the royal brothers, Enrique cannot allow the King to think he was trying to slay him after he accidentally cut the monarch's finger with a dagger.

Techniques—The drama is an ingenious interplay of fact and fiction in the working out of the main and reflector actions. Along with action involving the conjugal honor of Gutierre and Mencía (and Leonor and Gutierre), there is another reflector action on a similar theme that concerns the family honor of Prince Enrique and King Pedro. Calderón depicts Pedro the King as he was known in history as *el cruel* and also as *el justiciero* (the dispenser of justice). He is first seen as a dispenser of justice when he orders Enrique to cease courting a married woman since, even though he has royal blood in his veins, he is not above the King's justice. At the end of the play the monarch is depicted as *el cruel* when he gives tacit approval to the murder of Mencía and the marriage of the guilty party to another woman.

As the play unfolds, it assumes more and more the drama of a courtroom scene wherein both parties to a lawsuit are given a hearing, witnesses are called, and testimony is taken. When Enrique demands the right to speak in his own defense, the King refuses to listen to the whole truth, for fear that Gutierre, the plaintiff, who is hiding behind a screen to ascertain the true state of affairs between his wife and the Prince, may know that phase of the truth which will sully the honor of the royal household.

The King as the symbol of justice is called upon later by Leonor to restore her lost honor; she had suffered this outrage when Gutierre abandoned her and married Mencía. The monarch promises to "deal justice as justice should be dealt in this affair." [7] But first the King wishes to "hear the other party and his defense." The King promises to administer justice to all regardless of wealth or poverty.

Toward the end of Act Two when Gutierre scales the guarded wall, he finds his wife asleep and suspects she is waiting for someone. He realizes it is an "unjust thought . . . an infamous suspicion." This is in direct contrast to Mencía's attitude of unfounded suspicion in Act One when Gutierre wished to go to Seville to welcome the King, and his wife suspected his passion had been aroused by Leonor. To clear up his doubts and ascertain the truth, he extinguishes the light, disguises his voice, and awakens his wife. Mencía fails to recognize him in the darkness, and moreover she imagines that only the Prince would be so daring as to assault her honor furtively and clandestinely. Gutierre believes only a partial truth, for he seems inclined to discredit Mencía's remark that she wants to have the Prince slain on the spot to vindicate her honor. To add to Mencía's confusion and doubts, Gutierre again appears, after having gone back over the wall to return through the garden gate. Husband and wife dissimulate their true feelings and greet each other tenderly. Then Gutierre's speeches with their double meanings become apparently unintelligible to Mencía. In fact the dialogue in this section is partly in asides to express the true feelings of the couple. When Mencía accuses Gutierre of jealousy, the latter openly boasts he would tear out the heart from his guilty wife's body with his bare hands. But in the next moment he restrains himself, attributing his uncontrollable emotion to "this fiction of the mind."

In the scene early in Act Three in which Enrique is being questioned about his relations with Mencía, the King *thinks* he knows the true motive which impelled his brother to act the way he did. The King believes that the Prince is *inventing* the story to conceal his true motives to seize power. The Prince is thus condemned by his brother on circumstantial evidence just as Mencía will be condemned by her husband also on inconclusive evidence, evidence that shows only a partial truth. The hearing before the King reveals that Gutierre needs no tangible reason to confirm his suspicion of his wife's infidelity:

> . . . men like me
> Do not require to see: it is enough
> That to imagine, to suspect, to fancy,
> To have an inkling, entertain a doubt . . . .
> (Act Three)

The irony is compelling as the King, who is extolled as the symbol of justice, accepts Gutierre's explanation of his conduct, and is willing to allow a figment of his subject's imagination to stand for the truth. The King points to the dagger as a hieroglyph which has come to plead against Enrique with its tongue and spell out his guilt. When Enrique accidentally cuts the King's hand as he takes the dagger, the monarch misinterprets the act as a threat to his person; the audience of the day knew full well that the facts of history attested the enmity between the brothers. To preserve his escutcheon without blemish, the Prince decides to absent himself so that his brother may never suspect him of harboring so nefarious a scheme. Gutierre, who is hiding behind a screen, also misinterprets Enrique's motives, assuming it must be a guilty conscience that prompts the Prince to leave the court. After all, as the dramatist himself indicates, it is the trials of honor that are most perilous.

After Jacinta, a servant, reveals that the man in the garden could not possibly have been Enrique, Mencía's mental confusion and anguish increase as she awakens to the realization that the man must have been her own husband. In such a perturbed state of mind, she cannot distinguish truth from fiction. Although she still loves Enrique, she will do nothing to stain her honor or that of her husband. In her confused state of mind she readily accepts Jacinta's suggestion to write the Prince and urge him to remain in town. Her attitude here parallels that at the opening of the play when she begged Enrique to remain after his fall from a horse, out of fear for his health. Now she wants him to remain in deference to her health, i.e., her reputation which may be maligned if the Prince leaves and wagging tongues and idle gossipers seek to unearth a reason for his departure. Surprising her in the act of writing the incriminating epistle, Gutierre leaps to the conclusion that his wife is carrying on an affair with the Prince, and he needs no further supporting evidence to indicate where his duty lies. He has made up his mind that what he has seen is the truth; only the reader knows differently.

When Mencía becomes aware that a man is present, she swoons. Later, half delirious, as she recovers consciousness, again the ambient of a court of law is accentuated by her plea, "I am not guilty." Her husband's notation affixed to his wife's letter during the time she was unconscious is the "sentence . . . of death."

The King hears yet another witness for the defendant when Coquín the clown corroborates the testimony of Ludovico the bloodletter concerning the innocence of Mencía. Coquín speaks as a "veritable man of truth," and the emphasis here is on the thrice repeated "truth." Ironically enough, Coquín is the only one who has clearly perceived how Gutierre departed from the truth and was led astray by a mass of false appearances, suspicions, falsely confirmed jealousy and fallacious reports. As a reward for this information he begs the King to "suspend . . . legal action" against him for his failure to provoke laughter.

Later the King finds over the doorway the telltale mark of a bloody hand which convinces him of Gutierre's guilt. But Pedro is unable to take any action as Gutierre has so cleverly concealed his crime. The King as judge supreme is unable to render a "verdict" at the moment. Later the dramatist provides a way out when Leonor begs the monarch to force Gutierre to fulfill his promise and become her husband.

The view that the action of the play is like a lawsuit is enhanced by the dramatist's use of dialectics and casuistry. Mencía early in Act One tries to justify to Enrique her action in marrying Gutierre and argues that it was not deception. In Act Three Jacinta convinces Mencía by arguments that it might be prejudicial to her interest if Enrique left town at the critical moment, and Mencía, following her servant's advice, pens the self-incriminating letter. When Gutierre wishes to attend Prince Enrique and accompany him to Seville, Mencía accuses him of infidelity with the remark:

> who can doubt that Leonor has roused
> Your passion once again?
>
> (Act One)

To prove he still loves Mencía, Gutierre employs a metaphor, comparing Leonor to a star and Mencía to the sun. "Now listen to my argument," he says, and then applies the analogy to his relationship with Mencía. Again in Act Two Leonor accuses Arias as to some extent the cause of Gutierre's defection from his troth. If Arias persists in courting Leonor, the latter argues, it would justify the jilt and point the finger of guilt at Leonor and Arias. It would exonerate Gutierre and cast a double slur on Leonor's name. She reasons that she must never give Gutierre, the faithless fugitive, the opportunity to clear himself. These arguments and debates between characters resemble the agones of Greek tragedy.

The Theme of Honor and Tragedy—The problem of honor is psychological and has its roots deep in the human personality. For this reason it has had a tradition that reaches back into the remote past and extends down to our own day under various guises in different parts of the world, such as "saving face" or "reputation" or personal and family integrity. What will other people say about us if we are caught in a compromising situation and made the laughing-stock of the community?

The conviction of an innocent woman on the false charge of infidelity is shocking and the inhuman and barbarous cruelty of having her bled to death is offensive to the modern reader, especially of the Anglo-Saxon tradition. And it is made doubly so when the guilty ones go unpunished, and when Gutierre, the worst offender, is allowed to marry Leonor, the girl he originally loved. Mencía, the innocent victim, is sacrificed on the altar of "honor." Menéndez y Pelayo points out that the public would never have tolerated a "Christian" ending in which the husband pardoned the offense of the wife in matters of jealousy and adultery. And yet the idea of pardon is inherent in the meaning conveyed by the crucifix that hangs above Mencía's bed, as Professor Wilson has indicated. But that pardon is not to be obtained in this world; it is reserved for the next, and it is connected with the saving of her soul for which Gutierre allows her two hours.

The strictness of the honor code and a rigorous adherence to its principles provided the climate in which secrecy prevailed and deceit flourished. It is no wonder, therefore, that the theater of the period, which some critics have called a mirror of society, is full of escapades involving men and women seeking to pursue happiness but at the same time dissimulating their true feelings in order to avoid being caught in compromising situations.

To stain a person's honor was an act of shame. To remove the tarnish from one's soiled honor required the shedding of the offender's blood. It mattered not whether the offense was real or imaginary. The individual ultimately had to purify himself of the degradation, just as society also had to purify itself. This ceremony of purification for the restoration of the individual's lost honor assumed a ritualistic quality in consonance with the sacrifice of a scapegoat to propitiate an inscrutable and offended deity which we may call society. Thus the honor dramas, like the one-act religious pieces dealing with the Eucharist (the *autos sacramentales*), are supremely revelatory examples of the ritualistic side of Calderón's theater.

If we consider the honor question as ritual, this concept will be reinforced by considering also as ritual the tragic drama that unfolds. It has been shown by the Cambridge School of Classical Anthropologists that the form of Greek tragedy closely follows the ancient ritual of the seasonal gods. Some of the exponents of this school of thought maintain that the festival in honor of Dionysos, related primarily to the annual vegetation rites, also included other ceremonies like the assumption of manhood and intercessions for the welfare of the city and its citizens. Thus tragedy in this sense celebrates not only precarious individual growth but also that of the whole human race. In regard to our play, we see in what manner Gutierre protects himself and his honor, and how this attitude is supported not only by his second wife, who agrees to live under the same trying conditions, but also by the monarch as the representative of all the people. When the audience viewed the play, it was watching a kind of sacred struggle, in the issue of which all had a stake. It knew beforehand or intuited what the final outcome would be. It was witnessing a ritual in which the conclusion would always be the same; the details were the variables. As in a ceremony of purification, individual as well as collective honor was restored by the slaughter of the sacrificial lamb; in our play, Mencía, an innocent victim. Thus both the person offended and society were given a new lease on life and the traditional customs were preserved. Calderón, then, was following the dual tradition of the concepts of honor and of tragedy. But it is a peculiarly Spanish variety of tragedy based partly on Aristotle and partly on a kind of national and religious spirit already stylized for the *comedia* by Lope de Vega.

The ending has perplexed critics through the centuries. Is it immoral as Menéndez y Pelayo seems to believe? He points out that it is difficult to reconcile this ending with Calderón's tirades against the harsh laws of honor, the Church's approbation of his plays, and the usual moral tone of his theater in general. One explanation would have us remember that everybody knew that the King was punished later in history. This obviously goes beyond the limits of the play and disregards its esthetics.

In *Othello,* to which this play has often been compared, the protagonist experiences the shock of recognition when he discovers that Desdemona was faithful to him after all. He suffers deep remorse and such mental anguish that he commits suicide. The shock of recognition in our play is experienced not by the protagonist or any of the other characters, but by the audience witnessing the performance. The "new" kind of tragedy being written by seventeenth-century dramatists in Spain stems from their notion of Aristotle's concept of *admiratio* by which they mean surprise or astonishment based on incidents and actions that arouse pity and fear when they happen unexpectedly and resulting sometimes in what modern critics call tragic irony.

After Gutierre has convinced himself that Mencía has been unfaithful and must therefore die, he decides to show her a supreme example of his love, a "rare and strange / New form of loving-kindness, hitherto / Unheard of in the world before." This new aspect of compassion born, as he says, of his deep love, is not only ironic, it also injects a Christian note by affording her the opportunity of saving her soul, although she may lose her life. This idea and the cruel, barbarous and inhuman method of having her bled to death are integral parts of the tragedy designed to thrill and astound the theater-going public.

Another bit of evidence to sustain this point of view is found in Ludovico's speech to the King after he has bled Mencía to death. He remarks on

> . . . the strangeness and the shock
> Of an occurrence which I've taken part in—
> Than which the confused archives of the people
> Contain no prodigy of monstrous lore
> More to be wondered at.
>
> (Act Three)

The courtier Diego comments that "wonders and prodigies are in the air / Tonight." After Ludovico describes his bloody mission to the King, the latter is stunned by the "strongest prodigy / That ever happened on this earth." This prodigious act has also unnerved Coquín, who communicates his disturbance to the King. And when Gutierre informs the monarch of Mencía's death by bleeding, Pedro refers to it as

> This prodigy of sorrow and affright,
> This spectacle of wonder and despair,
> This symbol of misfortune.
>
> (Act Three)

The Physician of His Honor is a tragedy of awe in which the spectator or reader experiences a shock of recognition regarding the terribleness of the crime and the conditions under which it has been perpetrated. It is only within recent times that some critics have begun to consider this play a forceful condemnation of an honor code which, because of the nature of its principles, had to operate in secrecy and encouraged all manner of deceit in order to protect one's reputation in the eyes of a suspicious society more inclined to believe the worst rather than the best about people. Calderón's criticism is achieved so unobtrusively that it has gone almost unnoticed through the years. His singular contribution is the presentation of a situation in which the audience or reader is left to form his own opinion about what the play really means.

Calderón shows us the human limitations of his characters, and the inevitability of tragedy in human affairs. The King, the epitome of justice, unwittingly and indirectly supports injustice in order to protect his royal honor from being sullied. Neither he nor any of the other characters is interested in the "truth, the whole truth, and nothing but the truth," but all prefer partial truths which they insist on taking for the whole truth. Because we are human and our capacity to know the truth in all its ramifications is limited by our human nature, the chance for untruth and injustice is great, and it is more so under a rigid and severe code of morals which proved a breeding ground where deception and crime were spawned.

CHAPTER 10

The Mythological Plays

THE majority of Calderón's mythological plays belong to the latter part of his career when he was writing *autos sacramentales* and other dramatic works for the entertainment of the court.[1] The mythological plays make extensive use of elaborate stage effects, music and symbolism and they present some moral and psychological problem. The source is generally Ovid's *Metamorphoses* and the *Filosofía secreta* of Juan Pérez de Moya, but Calderón does not hesitate to institute changes in the original material to suit his purposes.

Susanne K. Langer, in her provocative book, views myh as a "new symbolic form, a mode of art" which serves to express ideas and meanings for which there had been no medium before.[2] With his genius for abstraction, Calderón could use the symbolism of myth to serve his purpose in dramatizing mankind's eternal struggle with the forces of evil. In *Prometheus' Statue* (*La estatua de Prometeo*) which we shall consider in this chapter, along with *Echo and Narcissus* (*Eco y Narciso*), the central idea is the struggle between reason and feeling carried out on two planes: the human and the mythological. The conflict between Minerva, goddess of Wisdom, and Palas, goddess of war, has been touched upon by Chapman in a helpful article.[3] Prometeo and Epimeteo represent two aspects of the dual nature of man, creature of reason and emotion.

I *Prometheus' Statue* (*La estatua de Prometeo*)

Plot Summary—Prometheus' Statue is Calderón's version of a Grecian myth. Prometeo and Epimeteo, although twin brothers, are of contrary inclinations: the former pursues letters, and the latter arms. Prometeo, an admirer of the goddess Minerva, fashions a statue of her, and the brothers then unite in an agreement to raise a temple to house the statue. But their newly-born accord is interrupted by the cry that a monster is abroad. Prometeo, seeking out the monster to destroy it, discovers it in the form of Minerva, who is disguised in animal skins. Casting off the skins, Minerva offers her aid to Prometeo to ascend into the heavens to seek out some of its mysteries.

While the two are absent on their celestial journey, Palas, the goddess of war and Minerva's twin sister, orders Epimeteo to destroy Prometeo's statue of Minerva, for Palas is jealous of her sister's growing popularity among the people. Epimeteo is torn between his loyalty to Minerva and to Palas.

With Minerva's aid, Prometeo, longing for a flame of Apolo's fire (Apolo is Minerva's brother), steals a ray of the sun (symbolic of the light of knowledge) from the chariot of the sun god, and tells Minerva he will consecrate it to her.

Disobeying Palas' order to destroy Minerva's statue, Epimeteo comes to carry it away. He plans to hide the statue where he may worship it in secret. As he approaches the cave where the statue is concealed, Prometeo appears with the dazzling ray of the sun in the form of a torch, and places it in the statue's hand. Warmed by the fire, the statue begins to show signs of life. As Prometeo makes off to carry the news to the people, Epimeteo is startled by the statue's power of speech. Prometeo returns to tell the statue that it is he who fashioned her and who placed the torch in her hand. Cries from within warn of conflict and war, but Minerva, before she leaves them, promises to teach the people the use of the fire which she holds in her hand. All exeunt.

Angered over Minerva's continuing popularity and Epimeteo's defection, Palas enlists the aid of Discordia to spread dissension among the people. Disguised as a peasant, Discordia provides a box which, when opened by Pandora (who is soon to appear as the statue of Minerva), will provide enmity between Prometeo and Epimeteo and their followers. When the box is opened, smoke, a natural consequence of fire, or more specifically of a fire that has been stolen, billows out.

Apolo, still disgruntled at having some of his fire stolen by Prometeo, is partly mollified by Minerva's argument that the fire took on added value when knowledge of it was spread among the people. Palas argues that since the fire was stolen, no good can result, as theft is always a vice. Apolo is not able to decide which of his sisters is right, and determines to play an impartial role between them.

Prometeo decides he has done wrong in having fashioned a statue to Minerva and in having stolen Apolo's fire. Minerva tries to reassure him. As he leaves, Epimeteo appears. Minerva disappears, leaving her statue in her place. Thinking that the statue is Pandora, Epimeteo gets ready to carry it off, but the real Pandora rebukes him for his worship of Minerva. The statue disappears as they talk and Epimeteo is puzzled, torn between reality and illusion. Thinking that Pandora is Minerva, he addresses her as such, then recognizes her by her voice. The two are still, of course, at cross purposes.

Preferring to reign through strategy rather than by armed conflict, Discordia descends rapidly to halt an imminent clash between the group headed by Prometeo and that of Epimeteo. The dissension between the groups ends in the arrest of Prometeo and Pandora at the hands of Epimeteo. Persuaded partly by Apolo's forgiveness of Prometeo for stealing his fire, Epimeteo has a change of conscience and is reconciled with his brother. Prometeo and Pandora decide to marry as the play closes.

Plot Structure and Techniques—The action of the play takes place on two levels: the human and the mythological. It concerns the basic struggle between good and evil, and the complexity of the issue when one attempts to distinguish clearly between the two. The conflict occurs both on the same level and between the two levels. First, there is the variance between two divergent outlooks on life, epitomized in the antagonism between two brothers, Prometeo, a student of philosophy and letters, and Epimeteo, a devotee of arms.[4] This quarrel is reflected on the mythological plane in their counterparts, Minerva and Palas. Second, a pseudo-love triangle touches the lives of Epimeteo, Minerva and Palas. Finally, the struggle is interiorized in both Prometeo and Epimeteo, and in their mythological analogues. At first, the two brothers are in accord in their devotion to Minerva, indicated in their desire to raise a temple to her memory. This harmony is disrupted, however, when a monster crosses the scene and stirs animosity between them.

The action straddles the two levels as Prometeo courts Minerva and Palas Epimeteo. The motivation of the mythological characters duplicates that which impels the human personages. With the connivance of Minerva, Prometeo steals a ray of Apolo's fire. Jealous of the popularity Minerva enjoys with the people, Palas orders Epimeteo to carry off Minerva's statue. The jealousy of mortals is also experienced by the gods. Palas enlists the aid of Discordia to sow enmity between the two brothers. Apolo supports Palas in unleashing discord among men as a means of revenge. The stolen flame of his fire has caused his prestige to diminish.

To complicate the action, Calderón employs the cross-over technique. By this Discordia intervenes in the affairs of mortals, causing Epimeteo to love the one who hates him, and Prometeo will hate the one who loves him. The woman in both instances is Pandora.

The use of disguises further knots the action and is at the root of the confusion due to the clash between appearance and reality. In her first appearance Minerva is garbed in animal skins, which is indicative of the animal side of her nature. Prometeo was not expecting her to be so arrayed and becomes confused. The allegorical figure, Discordia, arrives dressed as a peasant to sow the seeds of dissension.

In Act Three Prometeo and Pandora are masked so that people will not feel compassion toward them. But when the masks are removed, their temporary hatred of each other disappears and they feel a mutual pity.

Argumentation and debate also occur on the two levels. Epimeteo argues subtly before Minerva, asking her to scorn his love so that he may cherish her all the more. Rhetorical questions are sometimes used as pseudo-arguments involving a comparison. Minerva asks Jupiter: "is it not a worse crime to steal Jupiter's prerogatives than a flame of Apolo's fire?" In another scene both goddesses, Minerva and Palas, wrangle before Apolo over the crime of Prometeo.

The confusion caused by the disguises, deceit and mistaken identity operates on two other planes, sight and hearing. Prometeo is perplexed when he hears the "beast" speak since he sees her (Minerva) dressed in animal skins. Epimeteo and Merlín are puzzled over the speech emanating from Minerva's statue, which is called Pandora. Confusion also results from the cross-over technique whereby Prometeo appears to hate Pandora and Epimeteo seems to love the one who hates him, namely Pandora. The chaos that follows emanates from the clash between reality and illusion.

Evil apparently replaces good as Prometeo and Pandora are led away to the cave as prisoners. Epimeteo orders the masks removed so that Pandora may gaze on the one she loved and Prometeo may look on the one he hated. Palas and Discordia are jubilant. But Prometeo and Pandora experience mutual compassion and fall in love. This is a reversal of Prometeo's former attitude toward her.

Not to be outdone by Jupiter, Apolo decides to accede to Minerva's plea for pardon. The conventional ending of plural marriages closes the play: Merlín weds Libia and Prometeo marries Pandora.

The mingling of the mythological and the human lends a note of irony to the play. Calderón invests the gods with such human weaknesses as an animal-like nature, jealousy, the inability to distinguish between right and wrong and pride. This parody of the ancient gods is also found in other art forms like painting. One has only to recall Velázquez' treatment of "Mars" and "The Topers;" in the latter Bacchus appears surrounded by a number of vintage gatherers.

The abundance of such techniques as mistaken identity, cross purposes, disguises and the emphasis on the themes of love, jealousy and hate detract from the main theme of the play, at times almost obscuring it. Prometeo protects Pandora, not so much out of love, as because it is a gentleman's obligation to succour a lady in distress. Moreover, the groundwork for the marriage of Merlín and Libia is not prepared in advance and smacks of mere convention.

Symbol and Myth—Prometeo's inability to fathom the mission of his life has kept him hidden from all in the "uncultivated underbrush" of ignorance. He and his brother, although reared together, were of contrary inclinations, Epimeteo being a hunter, and Prometeo a reader of philosophy. Prometeo's thirst for knowledge led him to Syria where he studied astrology. Prior to his instruction in the "clear, pure light of learning," he had traversed "confused paths" like a "blind man stumbling in the dark." After his education, he returned to his native land to bring law and civilization to the barbarians. But when his own people accused him of being ambitious, he decided to withdraw to the solitude of the cave. Seeing how men repudiated knowledge and how the gods sought it, he came to worship Minerva most. To have her image constantly before him, he made a statue of her, "life-like and in symmetrical measurements." Just as the gods gave lustre to learning, so he tried to embellish his beautiful statue with flowers "so that they might hide the coarse material of clay." The statue of Minerva, endowed with life by Apolo's fire, represents hope; "he who gives knowledge, gives a voice to clay and light to the soul." In addition, the ignorance found on the human level in Prometeo, is also found on the mythological. Epimeteo asks, "cannot a deity which is envious also be ignorant?"

The cave not only symbolizes the dark labyrinth of ignorance; it may also be taken as a womb symbol. Prometeo is born into a new life by accepting the civilizing influences of learning.

Disguised in animal skins so that no one will recognize her, Minerva comes in search of Prometeo to dispel his doubts. Her attire as a wild beast represents the frenzied passion of mortal man and goddess. The monster in Calderón is usually a symbol of evil; the disguise worn by Minerva confuses Prometeo (as it does mankind) who sees in it the mingling of good and evil.

Apolo's fire represents the light of knowledge so desired by Prometeo for his people. Prometeo thus emerges as the champion of humanity; he operates in accordance with the notion that an uncommunicated good is not a good.

The Moral Problem—Calderón has dramatized not only the simple, basic struggle between good and evil; he has added depth and profundity by showing that it is not always easy to differentiate between the two. This he does in several ways. First, the problem is complicated when a good becomes tarnished by evil; when good commits a theft for the benefit of the human race. At the same time evil is made out to be not so bad when Discordia seeks (but for purely selfish motives) to enforce punishment against Prometeo for his crime, and against Minerva for being an accessory after the fact.[5] Second, Calderón dramatizes the confusion that results when both mortals and gods are unable to distinguish between appearance and reality; e.g., Prometeo's perplexity when he discovers that the wild beast is Minerva; Epimeteo's bewilderment in Act Two when he hears the statue speak; the inability of both brothers to distinguish Pandora from Minerva in Act Three; and the failure of Apolo and the people to fathom the true motives of Palas' arguments in Acts Two and Three.

The dénouement is brought about by another god, Apolo, for motives somewhat analogous to those which prompted Palas to order Epimeteo to destroy the statue of Minerva. Apolo pardons Prometeo, for he believed that Jupiter would ultimately forgive out of pity. In other words Apolo was not to be outdone by another god, nor was Palas able to endure the downgrading of her ego by permitting mankind to neglect her for Minerva.

On the human level, the man of letters (wisdom) triumphs over the man of arms (force). Calderón conceives of man as being endowed with a dual nature, and this split is represented by Prometeo, exemplifying the tendency toward reason, and Epimeteo, the tendency toward passion. The latter is thwarted every time he seeks to employ force and violence. His greatest frustration comes after he participates in plans for the annihilation of his brother and Pandora, and the two lovers are snatched from certain death by the intervention of Apolo.

II *Echo and Narcissus* (*Eco y Narciso*)

Echo and Narcissus, a mythological tragedy, has not received the attention it deserves by the critics, perhaps because many have regarded it as just another court spectacle written for the occasion of Princess Margarita's birthday.[6]

Plot Summary—Act One. Two shepherds, Febo and Silvio, are both in love with Eco, a nymph who is celebrating her birthday. Bato, a rustic, parodies the love-sick shepherds. All congratulate Eco, save Anteo, another shepherd, for he never knew how to express himself adequately.

In another part of the forest, Liríope prevents her son Narciso from leaving the cave and her protective custody because of his inexperience and naïveté. Both mother and son are dressed in animal skins. Anteo, who has been out hunting a birthday gift for Eco, comes upon Liríope who calls for help. Hearing his mother's cries, Narciso leaves the cave and calls on Nature to succour him.

In another change of scene Febo and Silvio are fighting over a ribbon that has fallen from Eco's hair. To end the dispute, she offers to give the ribbon to the one who will do her the greatest favor.

Anteo brings in Liríope. She recounts her unhappy life. An old wizard, Tiresias, has prophesied that she would give birth to a handsome boy and that a voice and a beauty would bring about his death. Hence she keeps him in a cave and invites all to see him.

Act Two. Liríope is dejected when she discovers that Narciso has left the cave. She suggests that only singing will bring him back. Confused by all the songs, Narciso is bewitched by the voice of Eco. He falls in love with her and wishes to embrace her.

Liríope orders Bato not to allow Narciso to speak with any shepherdess. She has also informed Narciso of his two greatest dangers: a beautiful woman and a beautiful voice.

Eco is disappointed when Narciso disdains her, and rejects the advances of both Febo and Silvio. She then sings of her love for Narciso whom she seizes by the hand and refuses to let go. Narciso struggles to free himself and Silvio attempts to help Eco. Both Narciso and Silvio fight but Eco implores them to desist. Febo stops the struggle because this is Eco's desire. Then he engages Silvio in a fight. The crowd enters, demanding an explanation which nobody gives.

Liríope realizes that Eco's beauty has overpowered Narciso and she appeals to heaven for help.

Act Three. Febo, Silvio and Anteo argue about love and friendship since all three are enamored of Eco. When they see Eco approaching, they greet her and leave. Eco is amazed at their coldness and indifference.

Narciso and Eco exchange greetings. Eco leaves singing; Narciso attempts to follow her, but his mother Liríope detains him. Liríope plans to put poison in Eco's path so that when the latter treads on it she will no longer be able to speak.

During the hunt Narciso wounds a stag whose blood stains the grass. The lad repairs to a pool to slake his thirst. He talks to his reflection in the water. Eco approaches to watch. Narciso sees Eco's image and talks to her. After a brief conversation, Eco is able to repeat only the last word or two spoken by Narciso. Chagrined, Eco decides to live deep in the forest away from human beings.

Sirene and Febo search for Eco. Narciso brings in musicians and Eco repeats off stage the last word of each line.

Liríope disillusions Narciso, pointing out to her son that he has fallen in love with his own reflection in the water. The mother sings that a voice and a beauty were the ruin of both. Eco is converted into air and Narciso into a flower. The clown Bato ends the play with the remark, "and there are probably fools who believe it."

Plot Structure and Techniques—The play opens with the secondary action in which a true love triangle is created: two shepherds Febo and Silvio are in love with Eco.[7] The main plot concerns Eco's love for Narciso and its frustration by the latter's mother Liríope in her well-intentioned but misguided attempt to prevent her son from becoming the victim of an adverse fate. Because of divergent viewpoints several conflicts will emerge: Narciso's desire for freedom and his mother's wish to keep him within the confines of the cave; Eco's attempt to foist her attentions on Narciso and Liríope's efforts to impede Eco's love for Narciso; and Narciso's inner clash over his inability to cope with life's problems.

The two actions are linked by the love of Eco for Narciso, and Eco's disdain of Febo and Silvio. There is also a kind of triangular love affair in the main action: Narciso will reject the love of Eco and his mother, Liríope.

Various parellels and contrasts are established throughout the play: the true love triangle of the secondary action is in antithetical balance with the pseudo-love triangle of the main action. Eco is as ignorant in matters of the heart as Narciso. Both Silvio and Febo in paired speeches extol the beauty of Arcadia. In contrast to the animals, Narciso is endowed with the power of speech, but he has, nevertheless, less freedom than they. The animal skins in which both Liríope and Narciso are garbed contrast with their human nature. Narciso's fear of confronting life with all its problems is in direct contrast to his earlier attitude in which he longed for freedom to lead his own life. Instead of fleeing his mother, he now inquires why she has forsaken him.

Eco expresses her dilemma in matters of love in polaric terms: should she speak or remain silent? This conflict over whether to remain silent or to speak out is also a problem for Liríope who had been trying for a long time to cover up her dishonor by remaining silent; now she decides to tell all. After her seduction, Tiresias cared for her. Like the Wise Old Man found so often in myth, he predicts that she will bear a male child whose end will be brought about by a voice and a beauty.

Calderón has set the problems of the two plots in the first act. He has introduced parts of the main plot and shown how they are to be interwoven with the secondary plot beginning in Act Two. Only one part of the conflict of the main action, that between Narciso and his mother, has been developed in Act One. The other part of this conflict will not be completed until Act Two where the two plots will be interwoven so completely that they will have been fused into a single, harmonious unit.

In Calderón's later years, music and singing along with other arts played an important part in the development of the plot. Mindful that music and singing will attract Narciso, her lost son, Liríope instructs the women to sing: Laura, Nise, Sirene and Eco. When Narciso is about to quench his thirst by drinking from the pool, he experiences an inner conflict based on lips (speaking) and ears (hearing).

Under the spell of Eros, Narciso casts his eyes on Eco and is overcome by a violent eruption of his emotions. He is seized by a mother-beloved conflict which will ultimately be one of the factors that causes the catastrophe.

Comic relief is provided by Bato, the clown, who parodies the actions of the love-sick characters. He expresses his opinion to the other shepherds and shepherdesses that mother and son are savage. When Sirene explains the love affair of Eco and Narciso as an example of the biological urge in terms of man and woman, Bato contends that "they are the world's worst savages." He further adds that women are wont to be pleased by "savages." He then goes on to enumerate the types of men that women are most prone to admire. This sequence not only affords comic relief; by contrast it underlines the serious theme of the destructive potential of love.

Imagery and Symbolism—Calderón has chosen to locate the action of the play in the bucolic ambient of Arcadia which he, like so many of his epoch, considered as the supreme archetype of a simple, natural and perfect existence. This concept finds artistic expression in the alternating verses of intense lyricism recited by Silvio and Febo extolling the natural beauty of the area with its lofty mountains soaring toward the clouds, its brilliant landscapes, its chattering birds and lowing cattle.

The tangled underbrush and the jagged cliffs that surround the cave where Liríope and her son dwell act as a wall restricting the freedom of Narciso who longs to join the birthday celebration in honor of Eco. Armed with bow and arrows, Liríope prevents Narciso from leaving the vicinity because of the danger from the all-consuming power of love. Narciso is unable to understand his mother's reasoning. He recounts the story of young birds who, shortly after birth, are expelled from the nest by the mother bird and left to shift for themselves. Next he relates how the lioness ejects the young whelps from the lair as soon as they are strong enough to fend for themselves. Then Narciso asks his mother why she denies him the gift of liberty which heaven grants to a bird and a beast. The rugged terrain harmonizes with the cruel nature of the mother in confining her son to the limits of the cave and its immediate environs.

The cave in which Narciso has been reared symbolizes his ignorance about life. The mother has broken the great chain of being which Nature grants to all its creatures, and this violation of a natural law portends only catastrophe for the hapless Narciso whose innate desire for female companionship is frustrated by an overbearing mother.

Later Narciso falls in love with his own image and ironically his mother takes him to task for his mistake when in reality she must share some of the burden of his ignorance in matters of love.

The cave may also be regarded as a womb symbol from which Narciso has just emerged, helpless as a new-born babe. His earlier cries for liberty may be compared to the kicking of the unborn child locked in the matrix. In direct antithesis to his longing for liberty is his speech of fear and frustration when he finds himself alone and unable to make his way through the maze called life. The pathetic inquiry is directed to his absent mother: "What am I to do alone in these mountains without you, not knowing who I am, nor how men live, since you have taught me nothing except to speak?"

The pool of water where Narciso intends to drink may be symbolic of the water of life where he may renew himself. At the same time, however, it is fraught with danger, for it is also a mirror symbol in which he sees the reflection of his own image and falls in love with his own beauty. This self-enamorment is a substitution for love toward the opposite sex. As Narciso talks to his image in the water, thinking it to be a goddess, Eco approaches to satisfy her curiosity. Her image too is reflected in the pool. Narciso is confused and wonders why the deity reflected in the water has two bodies. Eco tries to dispel Narciso's "ignorance" which is greater than her "pain," explaining that the water acts as a mirror. As she is about to reveal the identity of the "goddess" he admires in the water, she loses her power of speech and becomes only an echo. At this crucial moment Narciso seeks musicians to sing to the deity to whom he has surrendered "his being, his life and his soul." Thus the pool of water, as a reflector, can work for Narciso's good or for his harm, depending on his knowledge of how to use it.

The tragic tale of *Echo and Narcissus* is the result of the mistaken philosophy of a proud mother guided by self-interest and a sense of guilt and dishonor brought about by those natural forces she seeks to repress in her son, the fruit of an illicit union. Because of his isolation from society since birth and his ignorance of social intercourse, Narciso is unable to cope with the problems of life. His mother has taught him nothing about life outside the dark interior of the cave where he has learned only how to use the human endowment of speech. She has not instructed him in the facts of life and when he falls in love with Eco, his mother's unwise discipline and rigorous upbringing make it impossible for him to shake off these shackling bonds which hinder his self-realization and prevent his integration into society by marriage to one of its kind. In fact he falls in love with his own image reflected in a pool of water, mistaking it for a water sprite. He has become emotionally incapable of making Eco the object of his affection and the nymph whose love is left unrequited dies of a broken heart. The main action of the play is formed by a pseudo-love triangle with Narciso at the apex enamored by Eco in sexual love and restrained by the maternal love or possessiveness of Liríope.

Narciso's self-love may be traced directly to the unwholesome influence of the "terrible" mother who has deliberately reared her son in a cave isolated from the rest of the world and in a virtual state of ignorance concerning life and society.[8] Related to this problem are others involving the training and education of children for life, and their freedom from parental domination and abuse of authority in order to work out their own destiny. The mother, Liríope, has been motivated by partly selfish and partly altruistic reasons to rear her son in seclusion. She foolishly tries to hide Narciso, the fruit of her illicit love affair with one Céfiro, in order to protect the reputation. Morever she vainly tries to thwart the prophecy that her son's ruin will be caused by a voice and a beauty. Thus by isolation she attempts to prevent Narciso from succumbing to the power of love as she did. But she does not realize that love frustrated in one direction may find an outlet in another direction, e.g., self-love.

Since the illiterate and uneducated might consider the fable as truth, and also to satirize the stupidity of a man old enough to fall in love but incapable of distinguishing between a man and his reflection, Calderón puts into the mouth of the clown this line: "and there are probably fools who believe it." Frazer suggests that it was unlucky and even fatal to see one's own reflection.[9] The superstition flourished in various parts of the world and held that a person's reflection in water or in a mirror was his soul. The Greeks believed that the water spirits could drag a person's soul under water, thus causing him to perish.

But there is another aspect of the myth which does not appear in any of the known sources of the legend that I have consulted in Ovid and Pausanias. And this is Calderón's contribution to what otherwise might have been an insipid and mediocre dramatization of the mythological tale. That the dramatist was fully aware of his character's motivation is corroborated by the detailed account he has given concerning the reason why Narciso falls in love with his own image. Despite the moments of mirth and laughter occasioned by the jokes of the clown, and despite the repetitious allusions to Margarita's birthday, it seems to me that the real import of the play for the modern reader is the overriding power of the "terrible mother" image on the innocent and naive son and the tragic consequences of her action, her credence in the prophecy and her misapprehension. The main theme of unrequited love is directly dependent upon the repressive influence of the mother in warning her son about the danger of yielding to the passion of love.

CHAPTER 11

The Philosophical Plays

THE two philosophical plays of Calderón are *Life is a Dream* (*La vida es sueño*),[1] and *In This Life Everything is True and Everything False* (*En esta vida todo es verdad y todo mentira*). The latter play is based on Mira de Mescua's *The Wheel of Fortune* (*La rueda de la fortuna*). We shall consider here *La vida es sueño,* usually recognized as Calderón's finest play.

I *Life is a Dream* (*La vida es sueño*)

Plot Summary—Having been dishonored by the noble Astolfo, the lady Rosaura dons male garb and arrives in Poland in search of her faithless lover. She and her servant Clarín come upon the prison where Segismundo languishes. The two hapless companions in misery meet, and Segismundo delivers a long soliloquy on his loss of liberty. Clotaldo, Segismundo's warden and tutor, arrests Rosaura and Clarín for trespassing. Clotaldo soon recognizes the sword carried by Rosaura as his own. After hearing a part of the story, he realizes that she is his daughter, and that her honor problem is also his. However, he remains silent about his relationship to her.

In the meantime, Astolfo and Estrella, cousins, have come to the court to visit their uncle Basilio, the King, and to explore their chances of inheriting the kingdom. Basilio had imprisoned his son, Segismundo, because the child was born under an inauspicious horoscope and the King wanted to spare his country the rule of a tyrant.[2] But now that the question of succession has arisen, he confesses his doubts about the veracity of the prophecy, and has decided to subject the prince to a test. If the prince is prudent, sensible and benign, he will be permitted to rule, but if he shows himself proud, rash and cruel, he will be returned to prison and told that all was a dream.

Drugged into a deep sleep, the prince is carried to the palace. Awakening in the luxurious surroundings, Segismundo proceeds to enjoy himself, doing whatever his pleasure dictates, without regard for the feelings of other people. His animal nature gains the upper hand, and he even makes advances to Rosaura, with whom he has fallen in love. Finally, Basilio has Segismundo again drugged, and returned to the tower. Muffled against recognition, the King notes Segismundo's reaction as the prince regains consciousness in his prison. A change is slowly taking place as Segismundo uses his reason and becomes aware of the conflict between truth and illusion. He agrees to try to suppress his animal nature, his irascible appetite and his ambition, having been tutored by experience and a dream.

Angered by the prospect of a foreign ruler in their country, several soldiers storm the prison to free Segismundo. Having profited by his previous experience, the prince leaves the prison, wiser and more given to reflection than before. But he still wavers, and his final victory is delayed until he has learned definitely to conquer himself. The prophecy of the horoscope is fulfilled when Basilio surrenders and throws himself at his son's feet. After reproving his father for his unwise policies, Segismundo in turn prostrates himself at his father's feet and wins forgiveness. Thus Basilio, learning from his son the lessons of prudence, temperance, fortitude and justice, acclaims him worthy of governing. Segismundo, as ruler, clears Rosaura's honor by ordering Astolfo to marry her.

The Notion of Life as a Dream: The Philosophical Backgrounds of the Play—The idea that life is but a dream has its roots in the mists of the past. The Hindus, who emphasized life's instability and illusory nature, expressed the image of the dream in their writings to underline the ephemeral aspect of life. The Chinese through Buddhist morality suppress the ego and deny the existence of time, space and even of life itself. Life is considered a dream and man does not know whether he is asleep or awake. The Hebrews express similar ideas in *Job* X: 8 and *Isaiah* XXIV: 7–8.

The Greeks believed in the ego as the supreme gift the gods bestowed on man. They considered the vision of a sleeping man a revelation of the mysterious power of the gods. But the world of the senses was separated from the world of the spirit by a deep abyss. Plato, for whom the inner life was everything, was disturbed by the distance between attainable reality and ideal perfection. Heraclitus lamented the transcience of all earthly things and the impossibility of distinguishing truth from fiction.

Christianity views this world as a preparation for eternity, and life as a continual struggle against evil. Re-echoing the prophets of Israel, Christian writers attack the vanity and deceit of this world. Honor and glory are nothing more than vain dreams.

The Drama's Plot Structure—The main plot of *Life is a Dream* concerns the regeneration of Segismundo through a series of experiences in which he is placed in contact with society. Under these circumstances Basilio is to judge whether the prince is fit to rule; that is, whether Segismundo has learned how to curb his excessive pride and can be humble, prudent, temperate and just. Only then can he assume his responsibility as an individual, and as a prince.

The secondary plot treats of the recovery of a woman's honor. Rosaura had been deceived by Astolfo in the antecedent action. This plot serves to place her in contact with those who may be instrumental in helping her remove the stain to her honor: Clotaldo, her father, Astolfo, her seducer, Estrella who may become queen, and finally Segismundo in his future capacity as a ruler. The secondary plot, among other things, illuminates the main plot by accentuating the themes of deceit, life and death, honor and the dignity of the individual.[3] Moreover, both Rosaura and Segismundo are companions in misfortune and they need each other in order to extricate themselves from their respective predicaments. Rosaura inspires love and its attributes of respect, pity and esteem in Segismundo.[4] The prince in turn is responsible for restoring Rosaura's honor.

The play opens with a segment of the secondary action in which Rosaura enters in search of her seducer. When she comes upon the prison, the author places her in relation to Segismundo, the protagonist of the main action. Thus Calderón early indicates the direction the action will take in the later reaches of the play. Then throughout Act One he pieces together the segments of the two actions by establishing a relationship between characters.[5]

In Act Two the playwright alternates the two actions. The major part of this act is devoted to testing the attitudes and behavior of Segismundo toward his fellow men at court. At the same time that Segismundo is failing his tests, both Basilio and Clotaldo sound a series of warnings with advice on how to conduct oneself. Since the prince has not passed the tests, he is returned to prison. When he awakens, he remembers what he has "dreamed." Since he cannot resolve the discrepancy between dream and reality, he decides to suppress his animal nature, and be guided by reason in accord with the suggestions made by Clotaldo and Basilio.

The third act deals with the waning power of Basilio and the ascendancy of Segismundo's star on the political horizon. The prince's meteoric rise to power is ironic since, by a strange quirk of fate, he is installed in office by a mob whose only excuse is that it abhors foreign rulers. Then by experience Segismundo "learns" what he failed to learn before: how to utilize one's reason, dominate one's passions and embrace the virtues of prudence, temperance, fortitude and justice. The secondary action loses its identity as a separate action when Segismundo agrees to help Rosaura regain her honor.

The Thematic Complex—Like many of the masterpieces of the Spanish baroque period, *Life is a Dream* contains a cluster of themes which the reader must sort out and examine carefully in order to obtain a better understanding of the work. The themes are sometimes found in contrasting pairs and are interrelated: pride and humility, free-will and predestination, man and beast, freedom and imprisonment, love and hate, illusion and truth, life and death, honor and dishonor, light and darkness, and honesty and deception. It may be profitable to consider a few of the more important theme-pairs and to show their relationship to the major action of the play.

Freedom and Free Will. As Rosaura approaches the prison, she overhears Segismundo's lamentation over the loss of his freedom, one of man's most cherished privileges. The prince expresses bewilderment over the reason for his lack of liberty. He has already learned from his tutor Clotaldo that "man's greatest crime is to have been born," (obviously one way of expressing the doctrine of original sin). Segismundo finds this explanation inadequate and unsatisfactory. He contrasts himself with a bird, a beast, a fish and a stream; he has less freedom than they although of superior intellect. When he spies Rosaura, he is chagrined that anyone should find him in his present plight, and as a "man among beasts, and a beast among men," he threatens to attack her. Only the power of love prevents him from doing her bodily harm. Her beauty has awakened love in him and given him life, but without liberty life is really only death. Here and elsewhere Calderón has the protagonist confuse the idea of freedom with free will; or, to state it another way, he fails to distinguish between freedom and license. This is borne out by Segismundo's attempts in Act Two to impose his will on others; that is, he conceives of freedom and free will as the liberty to do whatever he desires regardless of the consequent loss of liberty to others.

Another aspect of the same thematic problem is the conflict between free will and predestination. The horoscope which Basilio had cast for his son had predicted that the prince would be a tyrant and would conquer his father. The prophecy is fulfilled, but not completely, for Segismundo learns self-control and the meaning of the dignity of the individual. Thus free will triumphs over predestination.

Deception. The theme of deception is widespread. It begins before the play opens with Astolfo's deception of Rosaura, and, prior to that, Clotaldo's seduction of Violante. Clotaldo is confused and bewildered when he recognizes the sword she wears as his. Later, when Rosaura discards her masculine attire, Clotaldo's confusion and consternation increase as he realizes that her honor problem is now his, since a father must be the guardian of the family honor. But he does not reveal his true identity to her at this time; a parallel is developed in the main action wherein Segismundo is not informed until Act Two that his father is Basilio, the King.

The theme of deceit is found in another aspect of the action between Astolfo and Estrella. The former has showered all kinds of flattering epithets upon Estrella who reproves him for his vile action (the use of meaningless flattery), more worthy of a beast than of a human being. His deceitful intention is exposed when Estrella discovers that he is carrying another woman's (Rosaura's) picture.

Another variation of the theme of deceit occurs in a segment of the sub-plot and involves Astolfo, Estrella and Rosaura. Masquerading as Astrea, a servant to Estrella, Rosaura is able to observe Astolfo's behavior and thwart a marriage between him and Estrella. She now employs some of the "deceit" she suffered at the hands of Astolfo. Refusing stubbornly to admit her true identity, she tells him one thing while conceding another. Finally, she demands the return of her picture which he has been wearing. When he refuses, a struggle ensues, just as Estrella returns. By a ruse, Rosaura regains her picture and succeeds in creating distrust in the minds of Estrella and Astolfo, thus alienating them from each other.

Perhaps the most efficacious use of the theme of deception occurs when Basilio forbids Clotaldo to disclose the identity of the prince's father. Then if Segismundo fails the test, he will be returned to prison with the explanation that all was a dream; this would be a deliberate lie. Basilio's reasoning is based on a good intention: if Segismundo should know today that Basilio is his father and tomorrow he should find himself back in prison, it is certain that, deeply disconsolate, he would despair. Basilio sounds the first of a series of warnings, echoed later by Clotaldo, which will play a partial role in the prince's regeneration: "consider well what I advise you; be humble and gentle, because you may perhaps be dreaming, although you think you are awake." The advice is correct but the reason adduced is a partial truth, and the use of "perhaps" serves to compound the confusion.

After Segismundo bitterly denounces his father's policy, the King, disillusioned, decides to return his son to prison, "where you may believe that all which has happened to you, since it was a good of this world, was a dream." This, of course, is a calculated falsehood. After Segismundo learns from Rosaura that his palace experience was not a dream, the effect is to leave the prince more confused than ever over his inability to distinguish dreams from truth, since they seem so much alike. The association of pleasure with a dream plants in his mind the notion that pleasure like dreams pass away. Since pleasures are ephemeral, he will hasten to pin his hope on those things which are eternal. This reasoning offers one of the most important moments of the play, because it is the turning point in Segismundo's behavior.

Life is a Dream. The theme that life is a dream does not become obvious until Act Two when Clotaldo has brought Segismundo to the palace. As the prince emerges from the influence of the soporific drug, he is amazed to find himself surrounded by luxury and attended by servants. He realizes that he is awake, and that what he sees is not a dream. Nevertheless he is confused and cries out: "Oh, heavens, disillusion me." This is exactly what he needs: to be awakened from the deception, or sleep. At this point he abandons further reflection on his situation, thinking only of self-indulgence "and let come what may."

After Segismundo has been returned to prison, the King comes to note the prince's reaction when Clotaldo awakens him. The dream, like life, has moments of rationality amid its greatest irrationality. In dreams, as in life, Segismundo oscillates from one extreme to another. A wise remark made earlier lingers in his subconscious, and with his emerging reason it has meaning for his conscious life, but since reason has not yet triumphed completely, Segismundo's irascible nature seeks revenge for past injustices. Speaking in his sleep, he mutters contradictory remarks: "a pious prince is he who castigates tyrants; let Clotaldo die by my hand; let my father kiss my feet."

When the prince is fully awake, he confides to Clotaldo that in the welter of doubts and confusion of the dream, there was only one reality for him: "I loved only one woman; this was true, I believe; everything else passed away except this."

Before departing, Clotaldo reminds the prince: "that even in dreams one should not fail to do good." These words have a profound effect on Segismundo, who agrees in principle to restrain his temper, fury and ambition as he recites the closing lines of the act. It now remains for the dramatist to subject the prince to another battery of tests to ascertain if he will put into practice what he has learned from experience, a dream, the advice and instruction of his elders, the beauty of a woman and the prospect of death.

As Act Three opens, a popular revolt against the foreigners Estrella and Astolfo sweeps Segismundo into power. Mindful of how past glory and pomp have vanished, the prince is more confused than ever in his new reality. Reluctantly he agrees to accept the honor, remembering first that even this new status may be a dream (as it was in Act Two when he suffered a disillusion); and second, all power must eventually be returned to its owner. Still shaken by his return to the prison ("a sepulchre"), he employs a kind of self-hypnosis, repeating Clotaldo's words: "that even in dreams one should not fail to do good."

Imagery and Symbolism[6]*—The Horse.* Rosaura's horse is called a violent hippogriff because of its great speed.[7] Its precipitous dash is also compared to that of a thunderbolt, a bird, a fish and finally to that of an animal without a natural instinct, i.e., one which is behaving in an unnatural way.

The runaway horse epitomizes all of Rosaura's impetuosity and mad dash for vengeance. She has no more control over the horse than she does over her emotions. The horse is still further compared to those of Phaethon, which, sensing the inexperience of their driver, burned up heaven and earth in their headlong dash.

When Clarín spies Rosaura mounted on a fast steed, he describes her breakneck speed in the conventional imagery of the four elements: the horse's body is the land, its soul the fire enclosed in its heart, its frothy saliva the sea, and its breath the air.

The Landscape. The setting of the rugged mountains, tangled underbrush, jagged rocks suggests Rosaura's emotional chaos.

Like the god Janus looking in both directions, the imagery of the runaway horse and the rugged landscape refer not only to Rosaura's lack of emotional equilibrium but also anticipate that of Segismundo who will soon be introduced.

The Prison. The rustic "palace" where Segismundo languishes imprisoned in the fetters of his mixed-up emotions is composed of boulders dislodged from the mountain above. The crude architecture of the prison insinuates the nature and character of the occupant. Because it was feared that the prince would be a ruthless tyrant, he was incarcerated in the wilderness far from the civilizing influence of the court and society.

The prison represents several symbols of different but related meaning. As Rosaura peers inside the open door, she sees the inky blackness of the prison where night is spawned. Then she hears the clanking of chains, reminiscent of a galley slave, or a soul in purgatory doing penance. To state it another way, the prison is like a sepulchre exuding an atmosphere of death and decay that can stand for the spiritual demise of Segismundo.

The blackness of the prison may also represent the darkness of the womb. Segismundo has to be "born" into the world of experience and society for which he has been ill prepared. After his failure at the palace, he returns to prison where he must undergo a change of his animal nature. This represents symbolically his return to the womb from which he must be "reborn" as a "new" individual. The protagonist must now fight the typical battle of all legendary heroes for rebirth. In some mythic stories the hero must fight his father, his mother or a monster. In the play Segismundo's major battle is with himself and his nature.

The Light. Inside Segismundo's prison cell the darkness is pierced by a dim light, suggestive of the prince's potentiality to improve his lot. The flickering candle is symbolic of "redeemable humanity," as Professor Wardropper has pointed out.[8]

In Act Three when Rosaura dashes precipitously across the countryside in search of Segismundo, she appears as a glowing light which blinds the prince. This is the light of truth, for it is Rosaura who reveals to Segismundo the truth of his palace experience, and also the truth about herself. She addresses him in terms of light, comparing him to a rising sun which restores life to the flowers. Segismundo represents her last hope for restoring her honor.

The Book. Calderón frequently develops the idea that heaven is a book for astrologers to read[9]. In his study of astrology Basilio has read about future events both adverse and favorable. Heaven is compared to a book of indelible paper, bound in blue, and with golden lines (stars and constellations) in which is written the destiny of man.

Character Delineation—Segismundo. The prince is portrayed as a child of nature whose upbringing has been shifted from his father to Clotaldo. When he is released from prison, the half-savage youth is bent on violence in order to satisfy his every whim and caprice. Perhaps too, there is an attitude of revenge for the lack of parental affection he so much needed during his formative years.

Under the tutelage of Clotaldo he has learned about the Christian religion, politics and rhetoric. But he has had no practical experience with life, no contact with society nor the responsibility of its burdens.

He longs for liberty which he argues is the right and privilege of everything created.

Like so many protagonists of baroque works, he suffers from an excessive pride. When Rosaura discovers him in prison, his pride is sorely wounded and he threatens her with bodily harm. If anyone thwarts the fulfillment of his pleasures, he also threatens him with injury and death. In his impetuosity he knocks Clotaldo to the ground when his tutor attempts to prevent Segismundo from forcing his attentions on Rosaura.

The prince lives in a kind of dream world of sensory pleasures at the palace. With his subsequent return to jail, he realizes that nothing is certain, least of all the pleasures of life.

From his first meeting with Rosaura, Segismundo succumbs to the power of love. But he fails to fathom its true meaning until after he has learned to dominate his passions.

As the play progresses, the prince learns to employ his power to reason. He also learns that an unbridled passion and an irascible nature can only lead him back to prison, which for him is the same as death because it means the loss of his freedom and his dignity as a human being. To control his passions, exercise his reason and assume his obligations become for Segismundo a matter of life and death.

Rosaura. She has more of the masculine aggressiveness than is usually associated with the feminine. At first, attired as a man to conceal her identity and her mission in Poland, she pursues her erstwhile lover, Astolfo, with the same haste with which he probably abandoned her.

She has compassion on Segismundo for his woes and feels an empathy with him since she has found somebody who is more wretched than she.

She is so adamant on clearing her honor that she will stop at nothing: masquerading as a man in pursuit of Astolfo, demanding aid of Clotaldo, and offering help to Segismundo in his fight with Basilio.

Basilio. The King is gravely concerned about the welfare of his country. He desires to spare it the rule of a tyrant.

He suffers pangs of conscience concerning the imprisonment of his son and the denial of his birthright. He reasons that it is not Christian charity to take from his son the right to inherit the throne, nor to become a tyrant himself by forcefully detaining him in prison.

Basilio's mistake was that he placed too much belief in astrology, a dubious science. He trusted too much in his wisdom and the knowledge of astrology. He also comes to realize that he treated his son like a beast by incarcerating him and by denying him the love of a father.

His realization of his mistakes occurs with Clarín's words before his death. They have a profound effect on the King. At the same time he becomes painfully aware of his impending fall from power. However, he is encouraged by Clotaldo's suggestion that a prudent man can overcome an adverse fate.

Astolfo. He is a seducer and a faithless lover who has abandoned Rosaura. He is something of an opportunist and wants to marry Estrella in order to inherit a share of the kingdom of Poland.

He is selfish and looks out after his own interests. He offers to guard the rear in order that Basilio may make good his escape. With the throne vacant Astolfo may become King.

Clotaldo. The tutor of Segismundo and father of Rosaura is one of the few characters of noble intent. He has been a father to the young prince and a faithful servant of Basilio.

Clotaldo serves as a catalytic agent who suggests to Segismundo that all may be a dream and that he ought to concern himself with doing good in order to merit eternal life. He points out that a prudent man can overcome an adverse fate.[10] He makes a similar suggestion to Basilio as the latter is about to suffer a humiliating defeat. Clotaldo then is depicted as a man of principles and ideals.

However, he does place his honor above that of his wronged daughter. He tries to avoid assuming her honor problem by offering her money to enter a convent. Then he will not be obliged to offend Astolfo to whom he owes his life.

Clarín. The clever, witty servant of Rosaura is under the impression that he can achieve everything he wants through the use of his wits. Jokingly he tries to flee death by hiding in a "safe" place, a vantage point from which to view the "fiesta" of the battle between the forces of Basilio and Segismundo. Before he dies, he remarks to Basilio that "fleeing death, I found it. There is no sure hiding place from death."

CHAPTER 12

Calderón's Minor Theater

I *The* Zarzuela

THE term *zarzuela* (musical comedy) derives from the Spanish word *zarza* (bramble) since the place where the performances were first given abounded in thick shrubbery with brambles. The wooded area near Madrid known as El Prado was originally the scene of venatic excursions for the cardinal-prince Fernando, brother of Philip IV. Here a rustic palace was constructed where Fernando and his retainers were entertained in the evening by companies of actors from Madrid. In time the district came to be known as La Zarzuela and the dramatic pieces that were represented there with music, singing and dancing were called *fiestas de la Zarzuela* and later *zarzuelas*.[1]

The four plays usually classified as *zarzuelas* are:

1. *The Garden of Falerina* (*El jardín de Falerina*), composed in 1648 and performed at the Royal Palace in Madrid. Of two acts, it was probably based on Boiardo's *Orlando innamorato* or on a play by Lope de Vega.
2. *The Gulf of the Sirens* (*El golfo de las sirenas*), composed in 1656, and first performed at La Zarzuela on January 17, 1657. It consists of one act, an Introduction and a jig.
3. *The Laurel of Apollo* (*El laurel de Apolo*), composed in 1657, and first performed not at La Zarzuela as originally planned, but at the Coliseo del Buen Retiro on March 4, 1658. In the first redaction it was of one act and an Introduction; it was of two acts and an Introduction in the final redaction.
4. *The Blush of the Rose* (*La purpura de la rosa*), composed in 1659, and first performed at the Coliseo del Buen Retiro on January 17, 1660 instead of at La Zarzuela as originally planned. It is of one act.

Calderón's *zarzuelas* contain many references to persons of the Spanish court, the events in which they participated and places they frequented.[2] They commemorated some special occasion, like a wedding, the birth of a prince or princess, a royal birthday, a visit by a distinguished guest, or the accession of a new monarch. The plot is generally taken from mythology, and the piece was performed with elaborate stage effects.

The *zarzuelas* are important as milestones in the evolution of what is now known as musical comedy.[3] Because they contain many courtly and dated allusions, extensive allegory and mythology, the *zarzuelas* hold only a limited and antiquarian interest for the modern reader. In a volume as brief as ours must be, there is not enough space for a more adequate consideration of their meaning for their time and place.

II *The* auto sacramental

It is generally agreed that Calderón was the most accomplished of all composers of the *auto sacramental.* This one-act religious piece, usually allegorical, which centered around the Eucharist, was performed either on carts in the street or in the plaza on the festival of Corpus Christi.

The *auto*, which grew out of the old morality and mystery plays where allegorical figures appeared, blossomed as an individual genre toward the end of the fifteenth century. The first *autos* were more simple in structure and manner of presentation than the later ones. Their original purpose was to dramatize the enactment and significance of the Last Supper that Christ shared with His disciples before His Crucifixion. The festival originated in the thirteenth century when Pope Urban IV urged Christendom to commemorate Corpus Christi. As time passed the later *autos* scarcely mentioned the mystery of transubstantiation and took on more the character of a sacramental farce.

With Calderón the *auto* reached its fullest flowering. Poetry was wedded to allegory and historical motifs were represented as symbols of human life. As Calderón advanced in years, his *autos* became more and more involved with theological problems and were endowed with more elaborate scenic effects.

The *autos* were written for an uneducated public which attended the Corpus festivities to be entertained, instructed and inspired. The use of allegorical figures like Beauty, Religion, etc., achieved an immediate and obvious significance that could not be obtained readily by the use of personal characters. Allegorical figures usually symbolized some abstract idea whose impact on the populace was direct. Furthermore, the use of allegorical figures continued a tradition dating from medieval days when they were included in the morality and mystery plays of western Europe.

Catholic Spain was the only country in western Europe where the metaphor of the *theatrum mundi,* flowing from classical and medieval sources, produced a living art form on the stage to express a theocentric concept of human life. As such, it was unique and continued in popularity until 1765 when Neo-classic critics persuaded the King to prohibit the performance of *autos* as detrimental to public morals and good taste.

Ever since Spain had to defend the Faith against the Moorish invaders and for the hundreds of years that followed, it has been staunchly Catholic. It was extremely devoted to the veneration of the Sacrament of the Altar. It was fond of ornate processions, and open air spectaculars (like *autos da fé,* and bullfights) celebrated with music and dances that acquired the air of ritual.

Every major city staged a new *auto* each year. Intense rivalry developed between cities for producing the finest and most elaborate *autos.* Well known authors were commissioned several months in advance to compose them. Lope de Vega lent much impetus to the genre when he provided the *autos* for Madrid. But Calderón far surpassed Lope in this type of religious drama; for thirty years he provided the municipality with its customary two *autos,* from 1651 to 1681.

It has been conjectured that the crowd of spectators who witnessed the ceremonies patiently waited to enjoy the comic portions of the *autos.* As in the *comedia,* a certain stylization crept into the *auto:* the prologue (*loa*), the fusion of the serious and the comic, the appearance and reappearance of certain stock characters like the clown, the suitor, and the esquire, the accompaniment of music, dances and interludes or farces.

Calderón's genius for synthesizing the abstract and the specific reaches lofty heights in the *auto sacramental.* He knew how to mingle the allegorical, the religious and the realistic by capturing the basic ideas of an issue and presenting them on several planes of communication at the same time to the enthusiastic satisfaction of his audience.

The themes of the *autos* were extracted from many sources: from the Bible, lives of the saints, religious legends, theology, folklore, history, from current events and mythology. Calderón became so versatile in this genre that he could select any theme and skilfully relate it to the significance of the Eucharist. Some of his best known *autos* are *King Belshazzar's Supper* (*La cena de Baltasar*), *The Great Theater of the World* (*El gran teatro del mundo*), *God, the Only Fortune* (*No hay más fortuna que Dios*), and *The Great Market of the World* (*El gran mercado del mundo*). We shall now examine one of his most popular *autos, The Great Theater of the World.*[4]

III *The Great Theater of the World* (*El gran teatro del mundo*)

Plot Summary—The manager of a company of players calls them together to take part in a play. The characters will be a Rich Man, a King, a Peasant, a Begger, Beauty and Wisdom. The World will provide the costumes and the props. The King receives a crown and a purple robe, Beauty a bouquet of flowers, the Rich Man jewels, Wisdom a hair-cloth shirt and a discipline, the Peasant a hoe, and the Beggar nothing.

The Law of Grace delivers the Prologue, stating the two duties of man: "Love your neighbor as yourself, and do good, for God is God."

In the first part of the "play," each character in turn expounds his attitude toward life. The second part of the "play" has as its purpose to ascertain if the characters see any social purpose in their lives and whether they are prepared to fulfill it. Before facing death, each character has one more chance to mend his ways.

At the conclusion of the "play," the World collects the costumes and props. The manager will distribute the rewards. Only those who have lived their lives in accordance with the theme set in the Prologue, that is, who have found some social purpose, will be invited to the manager's supper (the Holy Communion) in the Epilogue.

Analysis and Interpretation—*The Great Theater of the World* was probably written about 1645, according to Valbuena Prat, but it was not performed until 1649 when it was given in the theaters of Madrid from Corpus Christi until the end of September. The extended run attests to its popularity; this can be explained by the power of its message, the charm of its lyricism and the simplicity of its language. The play treats of man and his destiny in this life and the next.[5] It teaches how he is to conduct himself on earth if he is to merit eternal life. The manager, who is in reality God, summons the world into existence to set the stage for the drama of life. The action of the drama takes place on two levels: the one involves the unreality of *acting*, the other the reality of *living*. The main problem arises from the failure of the actors to distinguish between their real personality as human beings and their unreal personality as actors. The beauty of the world is only a reflection of the divine and can never attain the reality of eternity. Likewise, the beauty of the human body is ephemeral and passes with time, but the beauty of the soul may be perfected and attain eternal life. Life in this world is only a reflection of the real life into which we are born through death.

The manager, who knows what role in life each person can play best, distributes the parts. The actors are dependent upon the world only indirectly and upon God directly, for the world itself cannot exist without God. Each of the characters must work out his own salvation in accordance with a pre-ordained social pattern of life in which the good of the individual and the good of society are the same. According to Calderón there is no essential inequality in the different social positions. The individual must never make his occupation the main goal in life. That would be to acknowledge that one's personality is limited by one's position in life.

Another problem arising from the allegory is: how can there be a top-flight performance without rehearsals? But that is unimportant. What is important is that each individual try to avoid error. Each actor must be guided by the prompting of the author, by the conscience and Divine Revelation. After the World hands out the costumes, the play is ready to begin. The Law of Grace sings the theme of the play: "Love thy neighbor as thyself, and do good, for God is God."

Each character then expounds his attitude toward life, and we soon discover who has grasped the purpose of his existence. The fundamental moral problem of the play is mirrored in the conflict between Wisdom and Beauty. The latter sees beauty as an end in itself, whereas Wisdom sees the purpose of her existence as the glorification of God. The Rich Man is unaware of any social purpose, and regards his wealth as something to be spent only on himself. The Peasant can think only of the harshness of his lot and has a vindictive attitude toward those who are to buy the produce of his labor. The Beggar's attitude is one of resignation and he asks for patience to endure suffering. The King glories in his unlimited power, as he sees himself the absolute ruler of his subjects.

The first section of a play within a play ends here. The second part will determine more completely whether the characters see any social purpose in their lives and whether they are prepared to fulfill it. The Beggar asks for alms and the five characters react in five different ways. Beauty does not even hear him. The Rich Man turns him away. The King shifts his responsibility to his almsgiver. The Peasant offers him the hoe with which to work for a living. Only Wisdom gives him bread to sustain his life.

Before facing the prospect of death which turns out to be the immediate cause of repentance of those who have not completely identified themselves with mundane things, the characters will be given one more opportunity to save themselves. To beguile the tedium of the long journey of life, each character does not tell a tale; rather he discloses his innermost thoughts. Although the King reveals his great pride, he is not incapable of repentance because of his dependence upon God for right governance. Beauty struggles to avoid the admission of her perishable loveliness and death awakens her to the realization of her own disillusion. The Peasant's desire to leave his farm in better shape than it is in now shows he has a social purpose which singles him out as a morally superior character of the play. The Rich Man displays no right concept of life, thinking only of enjoyment. The Beggar is happy to die and abandon the sin of the earth into which he was born. Wisdom prepared for death in life and is ready to face the inevitable, having seen things in their proper focus.

When the World collects the costumes, the central idea of the play is stressed once more. The King, the Rich Man, and others who wished to keep the things of this world in death, could not see themselves as men but only as characters in a play. They are despoiled of all they hold dear. The Poor Man and Wisdom had no worldly attachments and for them death is merely the antechamber to a fuller life. The Eucharistic apotheosis with which the drama closes is an allegory of Heaven and the bridge between life and death.

The Great Theater of the World by Calderón may have provided Pirandello with the inspiration for his *Six Characters in Search of an Author* except that here it is in reverse: an author is in search of six characters.

CHAPTER 13

Calderón and the Critics

IF one can penetrate the thicket of formal and artificial language, the stylized metaphors, the point of honor, the national psychology, and the exaltation of Catholic Spain, there appear in Calderón the universal conflicts of human existence: the same preoccupation with the purpose of life, the confusion and bewilderment caused by the clash of appearance and reality, the never-ending battle between emotion and reason and the baffling enigma of death. Calderón had the ability to symbolize and abstract meaning, thus crystallizing it for all time.

After Calderón's death, Francisco Antonio de Bances Candamo, Antonio de Zamora, and José de Cañizares were the principal Spanish imitators in the late seventeenth and the eighteenth centuries. They continued to follow Calderón's technique of plot structure and Gongoristic style, often carrying the latter to inordinate extremes.

The main French imitators of Calderón during the Classical period were d'Ouville, Pierre Corneille, Scarron, Thomas Corneille and Boisrobert. They were fond of Calderón's complicated and entertaining intrigues and comic situations. The French reduced the asides, eliminated the descriptive passages and shortened the long tirades. However, they maintained the five acts, preferring the Classical tradition instead of the three acts of the Spanish. It is interesting to note that Calderón did not influence major French dramatists of the seventeenth century such as Racine and Molière except indirectly.

Ignacio Luzán in his *Poética* (1737) was severe in his criticism of Calderón's theater. Under the influence of French Neo-Classical rules, he bitterly assailed such "defects" as the violation of the unities, the lack of verisimilitude in the plot, the errors in geography, and the anachronisms, especially in the historical plays.

Nicolás Moratín saw in Calderón a corruptor of the theater and the creator of absurd and delirious plays. He and Clavijo brought successful pressure on the government to prohibit performances of the *autos sacramentales* in 1765. But in spite of this negative criticism, Calderón's plays continued to be performed for one reason, because the insipid Neo-Classical theater failed to maintain audience interest.

The Neo-Classical critics failed to perceive that the spontaneity, individuality and psychological realism which the seventeenth century *comedia* depicted could not flower when it was subjected to the rigid, unyielding rules of the ancients. Art was much more flexible than they thought, and could not be essayed successfully in accord with a code of inflexible rules. What they found particularly offensive were Calderón's errors in geography and history. They could not understand that Calderón was a poetic dramatist trying to portray the essential spirit of an historical account rather than a "photographic" reproduction, accurate in every detail. The "delirium" to which Moratín took exception can be found not only in some of Calderón's plays, such as *El mayor monstruo del mundo,* for example, but also in the theater of the world's greatest dramatist of all time, Shakespeare, and his *Othello;* the tragic heroine of both plays dies innocent.

At the same time that some schools of critics were attacking the *comedia,* others were lavishing high praise on it. Calderón's influence on German dramatists and critics was felt especially during the Romantic period. The Schlegel brothers, Friedrich and August Wilhelm, "re-discovered" Calderón, finding much in his theater that was akin to their romantic nature. They translated five of his plays in two volumes which appeared between 1803 and 1809. Goethe in his capacity as director of the theater at Weimar introduced *The Constant Prince* to the German public, who received it enthusiastically. Goethe was much intrigued by *The Daughter of the Air.*

Because of some points of similarity with Goethe's *Faust,* Calderón's *The Wonder-Working Magician,* more than any other play, captivated the German critics. Rosenkranz, a pupil of Hegel, penned an appreciation of the two works, exaggerating their similarities; the net effect was to enhance still further Calderón's popularity with the Germans.

The Germans did find some faults with Calderón's character depiction. It was Goethe who remarked that there was a certain sameness to the characters in Calderón's theater so that they all seemed like leaden bullets cast from the same mold. This may be true of the large number of Cloak-and-Sword plays (which account for almost half of his total dramatic output) where the opportunities for character portrayal are limited. Nevertheless, Calderón has left an album of unforgettable literary portraits. One thinks of Segismundo, Pedro Crespo, Semíramis, Cipriano, The Tetrarch, Henry VIII, Coriolanus and Eusebio, this last-named in *The Devotion of the Cross.*

In England the poet Shelley translated portions of *The Wonder-Working Magician*; he highly extolled *Absalom's Hair.* He was especially fond of the *autos* and once wrote, "I am bathing myself in the starry light of the *autos.*"

In the United States the poets James Russell Lowell and Henry Wadsworth Longfellow felt a close kinship with the dramatic poetry of Calderón. In *The Nightingale in the Study,* Lowell refers to the great dramatist as

> My Calderón, my nightingale,
> My Arab soul in Spanish feathers.

On the occasion of the bicentenary of Calderón's death, in 1881, the venerated scholar and critic, Marcelino Menéndez y Pelayo, published his *Calderón y su teatro* which exerted a strong influence on Calderonian criticism until well into the twentieth century. Menéndez attacked Calderón's theater for its use of symbols, patterns, ideas and affectation.[1] Though written in Menéndez' early years, it later carried all the weight of his great prestige as a scholar. Even in our own day some important Spanish scholars have been reluctant to praise Calderón.

For a long time the Golden Age *comedia* was considered largely an art of improvisation, of bombastic verses and unrelated sub-plots. It was not until about the first third of the twentieth century that any really serious studies of the structure and imagery of the *comedia* began to appear. This revaluation opened new avenues of understanding of the art and meaning of the *comedia* and cast fresh light on an important facet of Spanish literature. Many of the scholars listed in the Selected Bibliography, and others have contributed to this revitalized interest in the *comedia* in general and in Calderón in particular.

In Spain, the leading commentator is Angel Valbuena Prat; his work on the *autos,* the baroque, and on an overview of Calderón's theater is well known. His son, Angel Valbuena Briones, who teaches in the United States, has studied the honor plays. Eugenio Frutos Cortés has a volume on the philosophy of the *autos.*

The greatest impetus to the re-assessment of Calderón and his theater came from the British Isles in the late 1920's and early 1930's when a revival of interest in the baroque ushered in a new day for both Góngora and Calderón. At Cambridge University there was a new spirit of criticism which taught that all literary works should be subjected afresh to a close scrutiny. Edward M. Wilson started with his almost definitive study of the four elements in Calderón's imagery. He later followed with his interpretative studies of such plays as *El príncipe constante* and *La vida es sueño.* He has also examined the *autos* and the early editions of some of Calderón's plays.

A. A. Parker's monumental work on the allegorical drama is a brilliant elucidation of the *autos.* W. J. Entwistle and Albert E. Sloman have deepened our appreciation of the dramatist's craftsmanship and our understanding of the meaning and structure of various plays. C. A. Soons of Jamaica is interested in imagery and meaning. N. D. Shergold studies Vera Tassis and the early editions. Peter N. Dunn, Cyril A. Jones and A. I. Watson also have made significant contributions to Calderonian studies.

Among the German Hispanists, Ludwig Pfandl, Ernst Robert Curtius, Leo Spitzer and Helmut Hatzfeld have given us penetrating studies on Calderón's baroque style. Max Kommerell and Hans Flasche have added to our knowledge of Calderón's dramatic techniques. In France, Albert Camus translated *The Devotion to the Cross.*

In the United States, F. C. Hayes has studied the use of proverbs as titles and motives. Eunice Joiner Gates, under the influence of the revaluation of Góngora, has been attracted to Calderón. As was seen in an earlier chapter, Max Oppenheimer has a penetrating article on the baroque impasses in Calderón. William M. Whitby has worked with the structural symbolism of several plays. Sturgis E. Leavitt's enthusiasm for *The Mayor of Zalamea* has earned him the distinction of being named honorary mayor of Zalamea. Bruce W. Wardropper has done outstanding work on the *autos*, and has also given us some cogent and provocative analyses and interpretations. Edwin Honig and William E. Colford are succeeding in making Calderón better known to non-Spanish readers by their admirable translations. Arnold G. Reichenberger, A. D. Kosoff, Edward Glaser and J. H. Parker have also studied aspects of Calderón's theater. A Canadian, Harry W. Hilborn, has numerous studies on Calderón's use of verse forms.

The future of Calderonian studies in the Western world looks bright indeed as new scholars appear on the scene, and those already established in the field continue to broaden the ever expanding horizon of our knowledge, understanding and appreciation of Calderón's theater.

Lope de Vega founded the national theater of seventeenth century Spain and set the basic formula of the *comedia*—three acts in verse—which Calderón inherited and perfected. Calderón invented little that was new; he was successful in merging the dramatic and the poetic into one unified whole accompanied in some plays by several of the fine arts—music, dancing and painting—that gave those works the ring of a Wagnerian opera.

Calderón, like Lope, bowed to the tastes of the play-goers who demanded a fast-moving plot with themes like love, honor and faith which appealed to the emotions. They enjoyed the rhetorical flourishes, conceits and lyric charm of the beautiful verses. But double plots have long since been discarded along with ornate metaphors and pompous, euphuistic language, all of which tend to obscure the main point of a play rather than to focus attention on it.

Calderón's plays are marked by a certain stylization in his imagery and a fondness for continual flashing of balance and contrast in the arrangement of plots and in character portrayal. Many of the technical devices like complicated plots, hidden identities, disguises, sudden appearances and disappearances are worked out with such precision that they give the play an air of artificiality.

On the other hand, his achievements outweigh his limitations. There is a careful craftsmanship in the construction of his plots which are more tightly knit, as Professor Sloman has shown in his recent book wherein he analyzes the improvements made by Calderón over his models (Lope and Tirso). His images are richer in color and more elaborate; his verses are more polished and contain a lyric power that catapults them to the heights of space. His characters are delineated with more psychological penetration. Moreover, some of his plays are on a more intellectual level than Lope's. Since Calderón spent most of his life in the service of his monarch, his plays show the influence of the refinement and elegance of the Spanish court.

Notes and References

Chapter One

1. More information about the relationship between Calderón and Velázquez can be found in Carl Justi, *Diego Velázquez and His Times* (Philadelphia: Lippincott, 1889) and in E. W. Hesse, "Calderón and Velázquez," *Hispania*, XXXV (1952), pp. 74–82.

2. For a more detailed account of Gongorism, see Elisha K. Kane, *Gongorism and the Golden Age* (Chapel Hill, N.C.: Univ. of North Carolina Press, 1928.)

Chapter Two

1. The information which follows has been largely drawn from J. P. Wickersham Crawford, *The Spanish Drama Before Lope de Vega* (Philadelphia, 1922).

2. The material that follows is based largely on Sturgis E. Leavitt, "The Popular Appeal of Golden Age Drama in Spain," *University of North Carolina Extension Bulletin*, XXVIII (1949), pp. 7–15.

3. Arnold G. Reichenberger, "The Uniqueness of the *Comedia*," *Hispanic Review*, XXVII (1959), pp. 303–316.

4. Gerald E. Wade, "The Interpretation of the *Comedia*," *Bulletin of the Comediantes*, XI (Spring, 1959), pp. 1–6.

5. *Romanic Review*, XLIX (1958), pp. 3–11.

6. A. A. Parker, "The Approach to the Spanish Drama of the Golden Age," *Tulane Drama Review*, IV (Autumn, 1959), pp. 42–59.

Chapter Three

1. J. E. Varey and N. D. Shergold, "Datos históricos sobre los primeros teatros de Madrid: contratos de arriendo, 1587–1651." *Bulletin Hispanique*, LX (1958), pp. 73–95; LXII (1960), pp. 163–189, 286–325. See also N. D. Shergold and J. E. Varey, "Some Early Calderón Dates," *Bulletin of Hispanic Studies*, XXXVIII (1961), pp. 274–286; and H. A. Rennert, "Notes on the Chronology of the Spanish Drama," *Modern Language Review*, II (1906–1907), pp. 331–341 and III (1907–1908), pp. 43–55.

2. Much of the information on the early theater has been summarized from Hugo A. Rennert's *The Spanish Stage in the Time of Lope de Vega* (New York, 1909).

For the court theater, I have obtained my information from Emilio Cotarelo y Mori, *Ensayo sobre la vida y obra de D. Pedro Calderón de la Barca* (Madrid, 1924).

3. For a detailed account of the performance see *Comedias de D. Pedro Calderón de la Barca,* vol. VII, Ed. Juan Eugenio Hartzenbusch (Madrid, 1918), pp. 385–390.

Chapter Four

1. E. M. Wilson, "The Four Elements in the Imagery of Calderón," *Modern Language Review,* XXXI (1936), pp. 34–47.

2. Max Oppenheimer, Jr., "The Baroque Impasse in the Calderonian Drama," *PMLA,* LXV (1950), pp. 1146–1165.

3. The following are the most common meters used by Calderón:

Romance. This meter consists of an indeterminate number of lines usually of eight syllables with assonance (rhyming of vowels but not consonants) in the evenly-numbered lines. The line may have only seven syllables, in which case the last word of the line ends in a *verso agudo,* that is, with the accent on the last syllable. If the line has nine actual syllables, the last word ends in a *verso esdrújulo,* that is, with a graphic accent on the third syllable from the end.

Redondilla is the term applied to a stanza of four lines of eight syllables each and rhyming abba.

The *silva* is a verse form having an indeterminate number of lines of seven and eleven syllables in irregular order of alternation, and often rhyming in couplets.

The *décima* is a stanza of ten lines, eight syllables to the line, rhyming ababaccddc or abaabcdccd. If it rhymes abbaaccddc, it is called an *espinela,* in honor of its inventor, Vicente Espinel. There is usually a major pause at the end of the *espinela's* line four.

The *soneto* is a verse form of fourteen lines of eleven syllables and rhyming abbaabbacdecde. The lines are divided into two stanzas of four lines each, and two others of three lines each. As indicated, the two three-line stanzas may rhyme cde, cde, or they may rhyme otherwise in any possible combination.

The *octava* is a verse form of eight lines, eleven syllables to the line and rhyming abababcc.

The *quintilla* is a verse form of five lines, eight syllables to the line, with any possible rhyme except that no three consecutive lines may rhyme.

4. Ernst Robert Curtius, *European Literature and the Latin Middle*

Ages. Translated from the German by Willard R. Trask. (New York: Pantheon, 1953), p. 561.

5. Curtius, p. 345.

Chapter Five

1. *Three Plays by Calderón.* Edited with Introduction and Notes by George Tyler Northup. (Boston: Heath, 1926), p. xliii.

2. See my articles, "Court References in Calderón's *zarzuelas,*" *Hispanic Review,* XV (1947), pp. 365–377; and "Courtly Allusions in the Plays of Calderón," *PMLA,* LXV (1950), pp. 531–549. Albert E. Sloman in "Calderón and Falconry: A Note on Dramatic Language," *Romance Philology,* VI (1953), p. 302, points out that this lengthy speech by Félix is "unashamedly irrelevant." But he is also aware that it was part of "the original conception of the play . . . which is ingeniously symmetrical. . . ." As Sloman indicates, Calderón's problem in his early plays was to accommodate his exuberant lyrical style to the dramatic action.

Chapter Six

1. C. A. Jones has studied the concept of true honor in this play as contrasted with the conventional honor in Lope's play of the same title. See his study "Honor in *El alcalde de Zalamea,*" *Modern Language Review,* L (1955), pp. 444–449. For more on the subject of honor and its relation to life and literature, see C. A. Jones, "Honor in Spanish Golden Age Drama: Its Relation to Real Life and to Morals," *Bulletin of Hispanic Studies,* XXXV (1958), pp. 199–210, and George Tyler Northup, ed. *Three Plays by Calderón* (Boston: Heath, 1926), pp. xvi–xxiv, and Gustavo Correa, "El doble aspecto de la honra en el teatro del siglo XVII," *Hispanic Review,* XXVI (1958), pp. 99–107.

2. Ernest Mérimée and S. Griswold Morley, *A History of Spanish Literature* (New York: Holt, 1930), p. 376, condemn Isabel's speech: "What a pity that this splendid drama, written for the most part powerfully and swiftly, is disfigured here and there by intolerable conceptism, as in Isabel's confession!" On the other hand, James Fitzmaurice-Kelly in his *A History of Spanish Literature* (New York: Appleton, 1904), p. 331, quotes Edward Fitzgerald's remark about Isabel's speech as "worthy of the Greek Antigone."

Chapter Seven

1. Some representative plays are: *Dawn in Copacabana* (*La aurora en Copacabana*), *The Two Lovers of Heaven* (*Los dos amantes del cielo*), *The Great Prince of Fez* (*El gran príncipe de Fez*), *Absalom's*

Hair (*Los cabellos de Absalón*), *The Wonder-Working Magician* (*El mágico prodigioso*), *The Purgatory of St. Patrick* (*El purgatorio de San Patricio*), *The Devotion to the Cross* (*La devoción de la cruz*), and *The Constant Prince* (*El príncipe constante*).

2. Emilio Cotarelo y Mori, *Ensayo sobre la vida y obras de D. Pedro Calderón* (Madrid, 1924), p. 133.

3. A full account of the episode may be read in Cotarelo, op. cit., pp. 131–142.

4. *A Chronology of the Plays of D. Pedro Calderón de la Barca* (Toronto, 1938).

5. Albert E. Sloman, *The Sources of Calderón's El príncipe constante* (Oxford, 1950).

6. E. M. Wilson and W. J. Entwistle, "Calderón's *El príncipe constante:* Two Appreciations," *Modern Language Review,* XXXIV (1939), pp. 207–222.

7. A. E. Sloman, op. cit., p. 73.

8. Bruce W. Wardropper, "Christian and Moor in Calderón's *El príncipe constante,*" *Modern Language Review,* LIII (1958), pp. 512–520.

9. Y. Gulsoy and Jack H. Parker, "*El príncipe constante:* Drama barroco de la Contrarreforma," *Hispanófila,* No. 9 (1960), pp. 15–29.

10. *Le Baroque espagnol et Calderón de la Barca* (Amsterdam, 1951), pp. 17, 22.

11. "Calderón's *El príncipe constante:* Fénix's Role in the Ransom of Fernando's Body." *Bulletin of the Comediantes,* VIII (Spring, 1956), pp. 1–4.

12. *Los móviles de la Comedia. Primera Parte: "El príncipe constante" de Calderón de la Barca. Segunda Parte: Investigación y estudio crítico: Los móviles del protagonista.* (Mexico, 1957), passim.

13. Leo Spitzer, "The Figure of Fénix in Calderón's *El príncipe constante.*" Chapter 7 in *Critical Essays on the Theatre of Calderón.* Edited with an Introduction by Bruce W. Wardropper. (New York, 1965), pp. 137–160.

14. Marcelino Menéndez y Pelayo, *Calderón y su teatro,* cuarta edición corregida (Madrid, 1910), pp. 186–187.

15. Salvador de Madariaga, *Shelley and Calderón* (London, 1920), pp. 206–231.

16. A. A. Parker, *The Theology of the Devil in the Drama of Calderón* (London: Blackfriars, 1958), pp. 14–19.

17. Bruce W. Wardropper, "The Interplay of Wisdom and Saintliness in *El mágico prodigioso,*" *Hispanic Review,* XI (1943), pp. 116–123.

Chapter Eight

1. Among the outstanding historical plays are *The Siege of Breda* (*El sitio de Breda*), a canvas exalting the Spanish victory in the wars in Flanders, and a counterpart to the painting by Velázquez; *Love after Death* (*Amar después de la muerte*), a vivid story of the uprising of the Moriscos and their subjugation by John of Austria; *The Schism of England* (*La cisma de Inglaterra*), the English Reformation seen from the Catholic viewpoint; *The Weapons of Beauty* (*Las armas de la hermosura*), a picture of the Roman hero Coriolanus; *The Constant Prince* (*El príncipe constante*), a quasi-religious and historical piece.

2. The *de casibus* tragedies are so called because they deal with the fall from greatness, especially of rulers, or those filled with lust for power.

3. William M. Whitby in his unpublished doctoral dissertation, "Structural Symbolism in Two of Calderón's Plays," (Yale, 1954), sees Semíramis' insatiable ambition, which is expressed in terms of conquest of power, reflected in her outward appearance. He considers the chaos in the macrocosm a result of chaos in the microcosm.

Chapter Nine

1. Sherman Eoff, "The Sources of Calderón's *A secreto agravio, secreta venganza*," *Modern Philology*, XXVIII (1931), 297–311.

2. For a listing of the major appearances of this play in Spanish, see my edition of *El mayor monstruo los celos* (Madison: University of Wisconsin Press, 1955), pp. 8–9.

Long before Calderón's version, the story of Herod the Tetrarch and a husband's cruel jealousy and suspicion of his wife's infidelity had a been a familiar theme in western literature. It had its roots in the Bible and in the classical epoch when it was conventional in erotic Greek poetry. It appeared later in the person of Theseus, the violently jealous husband, in the *Hippolytus* of Euripides. Seneca's *Medea* loses something of the emotional impact of the Greek drama as it is more a study of criminal psychology than of suffering humanity. The theme became better known in Lodovico Dolce's *Mariana*, first performed in Venice in 1565. Lupercio Leonardo de Argensola treated it in *Alejandra*, written about 1581, and in the later reaches of the play, based it largely on the Dolce rendition. In adapting the Italian play, Argensola made several alterations: Mariana is entirely innocent of infidelity and Alejandra is unfaithful, at least in thought; but Argensola has retained much of the physical horror found in Dolce's play—stabbings, suicides, poisonings and murders. Tirso de

Molina also essayed the theme in *Life and Death of Herod* (*La vida y muerte de Herodes*).

3. For Lope de Vega's ideas on tragedy, see Edwin S. Morby, "Some Observations on *Tragedia* and *Tragicomedia* in Lope," *Hispanic Review,* XI (1943), pp. 185–209; and Charles David Ley, "Lope de Vega y la tragedia," *Clavileño,* I, No. 4 (julio-agosto, 1950), pp. 13–19.

4. The Greeks and Romans considered love an illness. Writers like Plutarch and Plato called love a "frenzy;" the latter in his *Symposium* tells how it spreads through the body and infects the spirit with malignant humors.

5. Jealousy is a powerful passion, yet without some share of it, the agreeable affection of love has difficulty in subsisting in its full force and violence. In Renaissance thinking jealousy was not considered a simple passion, but a compound one, made up of a kind of envy which in turn is a form of hatred. Although jealousy is not the same as love, it often springs from love. It has the suspicious quality of fear which is aroused when one sees another in possession of what one wants for himself alone, and it is akin to anger especially in its tendency toward revenge. Sexual love may turn from fear or suspicion to hate, frenzy, madness and despair. The origin of jealousy is partly in the mind's imagination.

Jealousy in its noble sense means a watchfulness and a care which amounts to zeal. In its pejorative sense it is the green-eyed monster of fiction. It can be appeased, though often temporarily, by arguments and proofs. Envy is often given as a synonym for jealousy. Usually envy is defined as the desire to acquire what is another's. Both jealousy and envy are united in our play: Herod is not only jealous of Mariana, but he is envious of Octavian's power. His thirst for power then is linked directly to his love of Mariana, for he thinks that he cannot maintain her affection unless he is Emperor, and is able to satisfy her every materialistic whim. By raising the passion of jealousy to the preeminent position, it swallows up that affection which it before nourished and increased. Too much jealousy extinguishes love.

6. "Poetry and Drama in Calderón's *El médico de su honra,*" *Romanic Review,* XLIX (1958), pp. 3–11.

7. The quotations are from the translation by Roy Campbell, *The Surgeon of His Honour* (Madison: University of Wisconsin Press, 1960).

Chapter Ten

1. Some of the most important mythological plays are: *Love, the Greatest Enchantment* (*El mayor encanto, amor*); *Echo and Narcissus* (*Eco y Narciso*); *Prometheus' Statue* (*La estatua de Prometeo*); *Son of the Sun* (*El hijo del sol*); *The Wild Beast, the Thunderbolt and the Stone* (*La fiera, el rayo y la piedra*); *Not Even Love is Free of Love* (*Ni amor se libra de amor*).

2. *Philosophy in a New Key* (New York: Mentor, 1948), p. 165.

3. W. G. Chapman, "Las comedias mitológicas de Calderón," *Revista de Literatura,* V (1954), pp. 35–67.

4. The arms and letters dispute was a favorite one in Spanish literature. Cervantes has Don Quijote discourse on arms and letters in Part I, Chapter 38.

5. Apolo's prestige sinks after a ray of his fire has been stolen by Minerva. He supports Palas in unleashing discord among men and opposes Minerva whose motto is "a good that is not communicated is not a perfect good." She argues that what she did would redound to Apolo's glory since the stolen fire took on added value when its knowledge was disseminated among the people.

Discordia's motto that "the best victory is a victory without bloodshed," is only a sham to conceal her true motive, which is to wreak vengeance on Prometeo and Pandora. A vulture is to eat out Prometeo's heart by day for stealing Apolo's fire. Pandora is to be burned alive in the fire Prometeo stole from Apolo and with which Pandora received life. Palas contends that "to steal in order to do good is not a virtue but a vice," and no good can result. Apolo in his indecision cannot make up his mind which goddess is right and so remains neutral.

6. See my study, "Courtly Allusions in the Plays of Calderón," *PMLA,* LXV (1950), pp. 543–544.

7. See my study, "Estructura e interpretación de una comedia de Calderón: *Eco y Narciso,*" *Boletín de la Biblioteca de Menéndez y Pelayo,* XXXIX (1963), pp. 57–72.

8. The psychological concept of the "terrible mother" is discussed by C. G. Jung in his remarkable work, *The Psychology of the Unconscious,* Trans. B. M. Hinkle (New York, 1952), passim. He shows the influence of the domineering mother "of whom many traces are found in mythology." See especially pp. 243 and 367.

See my study, "The 'Terrible Mother' Image in Calderón's *Eco y Narciso,*" *Romance Notes,* I, #2 (Spring, 1960), pp. 1–4.

9. Sir James G. Frazer, *The Golden Bough: A Study in Magic and Religion,* abridged edition (New York, 1958), pp. 222–223.

Chapter Eleven

1. Two recent Spanish editions of the play are *Calderón's* La vida es sueño, ed. Albert E. Sloman. (Manchester: Manchester University Press, 1961), and *Calderón: La vida es sueño,* ed. Everett W. Hesse. (New York: Scribner's, 1961). A recent English translation is by William E. Colford, *Calderón: Life is a Dream.* (Great Neck, New York: Barron's Educational Series, 1958).

2. Peter N. Dunn has a study of "The Horoscope Motif in *La vida es sueño,*" *Atlante,* I, #4 (1953), pp. 187–201.

3. The eminent Spanish scholar and critic, Marcelino Menéndez y Pelayo, regarded the play's sub-plot as a strange intrigue wrapped around the main plot like a parasitical plant. See his *Calderón y su teatro* (Madrid, 1910), p. 278. This adverse criticism was repeated by others until it was demolished by E. M. Wilson, who succeeded in showing its relation to the main action. See his study *"La vida es sueño,"* in *Revista de la Universidad de Buenos Aires,* Tercera época, Año IV, Nos. 3 y 4 (1946), pp. 61–78.

4. Among the critics who have stressed the importance of Rosaura's role in the conversion of Segismundo are: Edward M. Wilson, op. cit.; Federico Michele Sciacca, "Verdad y sueño de *La vida es sueño,* de Calderón de la Barca," *Clavileño,* Año 1, núm. 2 (mayo-abril, 1950), pp. 1–9; Albert E. Sloman, "The Structure of Calderón's *La vida es sueño,*" *Modern Language Review,* XLVIII (1953), pp. 293–300; and more recently William M. Whitby, "Rosaura's Role in the Structure of *La vida es sueño,*" *Hispanic Review,* XXVIII (1960), pp. 16–27. Elsewhere I have tried to place Rosaura in proper perspective. See my forthcoming study, "El motivo del sueño en *La vida es sueño.*" In another place I have considered the factors in Segismundo's conversion. See my edition, supra, pp. 35–36.

5. Another way of looking at Act One is to divide the action into two parts: the first presents the moral and emotional problems of Rosaura and Segismundo; the second provides the background information regarding the birth and horoscope of the prince together with the political and moral problems of Basilio.

6. See my article, "Some Observations on Imagery in *La vida es sueño,*" *Hispania,* XLIX (1966), pp. 421–429.

7. William M. Whitby in his unpublished doctoral dissertation, "Structural Symbolism in Two Plays of Pedro Calderón de la Barca," (Yale, 1954), states that the word hippogriff suggests the theme of two natures.

8. Bruce W. Wardropper, "Apenas llega cuando llega a penas," *Modern Philology,* LVII (1960), pp. 240–244.

9. See Ernst Robert Curtius, *European Literature and the Latin Middle Ages.* Translated from the German by Willard R. Trask. (New York: Pantheon, 1953), Chapter 16, "The Book as Symbol," especially pp. 344–345.

10. The notion that the stars merely inclined the will but did not force it was of common occurrence in the drama of Calderón's time. See Frank G. Halstead's studies: "The Attitude of Lope de Vega Toward Astrology and Astronomy," *Hispanic Review,* VII (1939), pp. 205–219, and "The Attitude of Tirso de Molina Toward Astrology," *Hispanic Review,* IX (1941), pp. 417–439.

Chapter Twelve

1. E. Cotarelo y Mori, *Historia de la zarzuela* (Madrid, 1934), p. 43.

2. Details will be found in my studies, "Court References in Calderón's *zarzuelas,*" *Hispanic Review,* XV (1947), pp. 365–377, and "Courtly Allusions in the Plays of Calderón," *PMLA,* LXV (1950), pp. 531–549.

3. For a more detailed account of the development of the *zarzuela,* see Gilbert Chase, *The Music of Spain* (New York: Norton, 1941).

4. For an account of the *theatrum mundi* concept, see Ernst Robert Curtius, *European Literature and the Latin Middle Ages* (New York: Pantheon, 1953), pp. 138–144. There Curtius specifically refers to Calderón, and to his influence on the rejuvenation of the theocentric drama in our time, principally on Hofmannsthal's *Jedermann* (1911), a "play of the death of the rich man."

5. The best interpretative study of this *auto* is by A. A. Parker, *The Allegorical Drama of Calderón* (Oxford and London: Dolphin, 1943), pp. 110–155.

Chapter Thirteen

1. Bruce W. Wardropper, "Menéndez Pelayo on Calderón," *Criticism,* VII (1965), pp. 363–372.

Selected Bibliography

Early Volumes of Plays

Five volumes, or *Partes,* of the plays were published in Calderón's lifetime as the *First Part* (*Primera Parte*), the *Second Part* (*Segunda Parte*), etc., in 1636, 1637, 1664, 1672 and 1677 respectively. The first four were published in Madrid, the fifth in Barcelona. María Quiñones printed the first two, Domingo García Morrás the third, Ioseph Fernández de Buendía the fourth, Antonio la Caballería the fifth. Each volume has the twelve plays usually found in any volume of *comedias* published in the seventeenth century except that the fifth volume has only ten. Of the ten, Calderón, who had not authorized any one of the five volumes, disowned four plays, perhaps because he failed to recognize their altered titles. Of the four he disowned, two are not his.

After Calderón's death, Juan de Vera Tassis y Villarroel undertook the publication of the great dramatist's plays, beginning with the *True Fifth Part* (*Verdadera quinta parte de comedias del célebre poeta español don Pedro Calderón de la Barca*), Madrid: Viuda de Blas de Villanueva, 1682). In 1683 Vera Tassis published in Madrid a *Sixth* and a *Seventh Part,* in 1684 an *Eighth Part,* all printed by Francisco Sanz. In 1685 Vera Tassis decided to start over with the *First Part,* and in 1686, 1687, 1688 and 1691 he published the *Second, Third, Fourth* and *Fifth Parts* respectively. All contained twelve plays each and were printed in Madrid by Francisco Sanz. A *Tenth Part* promised by Vera Tassis failed to appear because of his death.

Since the nine *Parts* have a total of one hundred eight plays, limitations of space forbid the listing of the titles. These can be read in the Keil and Hartzenbusch editions named below. Some of Calderón's plays were also published in the two great collections of the seventeenth century known as "*Diferentes*" and the "*Escogidas.*" For a complete listing, see Everett W. Hesse, "The Publication of Calderón's Plays in the Seventeenth Century," *Philological Quarterly,* XXVII (1948), pp. 37–51.

Three Modern Collections

Las comedias de D. Pedro Calderón de la Barca. Ed. Juan Jorge Keil. 4 vols. (Leipzig: Ernest Fleischer, 1827–1830). A neatly printed edition now hard to find.

Comedias de Calderón de la Barca. Biblioteca de Autores Españoles. Ed. Juan Eugenio Hartzenbusch. 4 vols. (Madrid: Rivadeneyra, 1848). Vol. II, 1849; Vol. III, 1849; Vol. IV, 1850. One of the most accessible editions of Calderón's plays. Reprinted in recent years.

Obras completas de Calderón de la Barca (comedias). 2 vols. Vol. I edited by Luis Astrana Marín. (Madrid: Aguilar, 1945). Has the texts of forty plays based on first editions and manuscripts. Vol. II edited by Angel Valbuena Briones. (Madrid: Aguilar, 1956). Fifty-two plays. A useful and convenient edition.

Editions of the Autos sacramentales

Autos sacramentales, alegóricos e historiales . . . (Madrid: Joseph Fernández de Buendía, 1677). This volume contains twelve *autos.*

Autos sacramentales . . . Six volumes. (Madrid: Pando y Mier, 1717). Contains seventy-two *autos.* They have been listed, classified and analyzed by Angel Valbuena Prat in "Los autos sacramentales de Calderón: clasificación y análisis," *Revue Hispanique,* LXI (1924), pp. 1–302.

Autos sacramentales . . . Six volumes. Ed. J. Fernández Apontes. Madrid: Viuda de Manuel Fernández, 1760–1763. Seventy-three *autos* including the one Calderón was writing at the time of his death.

Obras completas. Vol. III. Recopilación, prólogo y notas por Angel Valbuena Prat. (Madrid: Aguilar, 1952). A handy and useful volume.

Biography and Bibliography

HERMAN W. BREYMANN, *Calderón Studien—die Calderón Literatur* (München und Berlin: R. Oldenburg, 1905). A valuable catalogue which now needs to be completed and brought up to date.

EMILIO COTARELO Y MORI, *Ensayo sobre la vida y obras de Calderón,* (Madrid: Revista de Archivos, Bibliotecas y Museos, 1924). The most nearly definitive study on Calderón's life and works.

EUGENIO FRUTOS CORTÉS, *Calderón de la Barca,* (Madrid: Labor, 1949). A brief study of Calderón's life and works together with an anthology of his dramatic poetry.

ARNOLD G. REICHENBERGER, "Two Important Spanish *Comedia* Collections," *Bulletin of the Comediantes,* VIII (Spring, 1956), pp. 6–7. (On the acquisition by the University of Pennsylvania libary of 42 *partes* of the "*Escogidas*" collection, 1652–1704, and 24 volumes of *comedias sueltas.*)

General Studies on Calderón

W. G. CHAPMAN, "Las comedias mitológicas de Calderón," *Revista de Literatura,* V (1954), pp. 35–67. An excellent analysis of Calderón's mythological plays.

A. L. CONSTANDSE, *Le Baroque espagnol et Calderón de la Barca* (Amsterdam: Plus Ultra, 1951). Classifies the baroque as the purest expression of Spain's anguish and of its vitality with Calderón as its chief exponent.

EUNICE J. GATES, "Proverbs in the Plays of Calderón," *Romanic Review,* XXXVIII (1947), pp. 203–215. Some of Calderón's best and most famous plays bear proverbs as titles.

F. C. HAYES, "The Use of Proverbs as Titles and Motives in the '*Siglo de Oro*' Drama: Calderón," *Hispanic Review,* XV (1947), pp. 453–463. Calderón used some twenty-four proverbs as titles for plays.

EVERETT W. HESSE, *The Vera Tassis Text of Calderón's Plays, Parts I-IV,* (Mexico: Privately Printed, 1941). Points out the arbitrary changes made by Calderón's first editor, Vera Tassis.

——— "Court References in Calderón's *zarzuelas,*" *Hispanic Review,* XV (1947), pp. 365–377. The courtly allusions were usually found in the *loa* (prologue), and flattered royalty or heralded some special event.

——— "The First and Second Editions of Calderón's *Cuarta parte,*" *Hispanic Review,* XVI (1948), pp. 209–237. Analysis of the textual changes in the second edition showing the intervention of Calderón himself.

——— "Courtly Allusions in the Plays of Calderón," *PMLA,* LXV (1950), pp. 531–549. References to King Philip IV and members of the Royal Family.

——— "Calderón and Velázquez," *Hispania,* XXXV (1952), pp. 74–82. Similarities in theme, style and techniques of the great artists and their achievements.

——— "La dialéctica y el casuismo en Calderón," *Estudios,* IX (septiembre–diciembre, 1953), pp. 517–531. Calderón uses rationalism not in search of truth but as a vehicle to develop dramatic conflict.

——— "Calderón's Popularity in the Spanish Indies," *Hispanic Review,* XXIII (1955), pp. 12–27. Examination of records giving dates of performances, and names of plays performed in Latin America during the colonial period.

HARRY W. HILBORN, *A Chronology of the Plays of D. Pedro Calderón de la Barca,* (Toronto: University of Toronto Press, 1938). Establishes the chronology of the plays and *autos* on the basis of a study of the proportion of the various types of verse forms.

SALVADOR DE MADARIAGA, *Shelley and Calderón and Other Essays on English and Spanish Poetry,* (London: Constable, 1920). Shelley's fondness for Calderón in his translation of certain portions of scenes from famous plays.

MARCELINO MENÉNDEZ Y PELAYO, *Calderón y su teatro,* (Madrid: Revista de Archivos, 1881). A series of lectures given by the distinguished critic on the bicentenary of Calderón's death. Menéndez later repudiated some of the ideas contained herein.

MAX OPPENHEIMER, JR., "The Baroque Impasse in the Calderonian Drama," *PMLA,* LXV (1950), pp. 1146–1165. Calderón's characters are driven by emotional wants to seek a self-expression in an illusory but harmonious fusion of discordant elements commonly called the Baroque.

A. A. PARKER, *The Theology of the Devil in the Drama of Calderón,* (London: Blackfriars Publications, 1958). Discusses the significance of the Devil in *El mágico prodigioso* and *El Josef de las Mujeres.*

N. D. SHERGOLD, "Calderón and Vera Tassis," *Hispanic Review,* XXIII (1955), pp. 212–218. Considers the changes made by Vera Tassis in the stage directions, and suggests that Calderón himself may have had a hand in the revision.

RAMÓN SILVA, "The Religious Dramas of Calderón," *Bulletin of Spanish Studies,* XV (1938), pp. 172–195. An excellent study; well documented. Reprinted in *Spanish Golden Age Poetry and Drama,* ed. E. A. Peers, (Liverpool: University of Liverpool Press, 1946).

A. E. SLOMAN, *The Dramatic Craftsmanship of Calderón: His Use of Earlier Plays,* (Oxford: Dolphin, 1958). An analysis of eight plays by Calderón. An outstanding study.

S. SAMUEL TRIFILO, "Influencias calderonianas en el drama de Zamora y de Cañizares," *Hispanófila,* IV (enero, 1961), pp. 39–46. Calderón's influence on two minor dramatists of the late seventeenth century.

ANGEL VALBUENA BRIONES, "El concepto del hado en el teatro de Calderón," *Bulletin Hispanique,* LXIII (1961), pp. 48–53. Fate in Calderón is the force which rules those instincts and inclinations that can control human actions and lead to catastrophe.

——— *Perspectiva crítica de los dramas de Calderón,* (Madrid-Mexico-Pamplona, 1965).

ANGEL VALBUENA PRAT, *Calderón, su personalidad, su arte dramático, su estilo y sus obras,* (Barcelona: Juventud, 1941). A basic overview of Calderón's dramatic style and personality. Valbuena studies briefly several plays in the various categories of Calderón's theater.

BRUCE W. WARDROPPER, "Calderón's Comedy and His Serious Sense of Life," in *Hispanic Studies in Honor of Nicholson B. Adams.* Eds. John Esten Keller and Karl-Ludwig Selig. (Chapel Hill, 1966). Deals with *Casa con dos puertas* as one of Calderón's best comedies and shows how the author's vision of the world lies behind his comedy just as behind his tragedy.

LUCY E. WEIR, *The Ideas Embodied in the Religious Drama of Calderón,* (Lincoln: University of Nebraska, 1940). A study of the *autos* and those plays dealing with Biblical and historical themes, Roman Catholic dogma, free-will, and the omnipotence of God.

E. M. WILSON, "The Four Elements in the Imagery of Calderón," *Modern Language Review,* XXXI (1936), pp. 34–47. A nearly definitive study on Calderón's use of the four basic elements of earth, air, fire and water.

——— "Calderón and the Stage Censor in the Seventeenth Century: A Provisional Study," *Symposium,* (Fall, 1961), pp. 165–184. Censors cut profane or irreverent allusions, immoral or heretical references. Calderón praised as a Christian moralist.

Studies on Individual Plays

The Mayor of Zalamea (El alcalde de Zalamea)

PETER N. DUNN, "Patrimonio del alma," *Bulletin of Hispanic Studies,* XLI (1964), pp. 78–85. Explains how all the characters are primarily concerned with their "rights," and how all have a different concept of honor circumscribed by their own personal interest.

C. A. JONES, "Honor in *El alcalde de Zalamea," Modern Language Review,* L (1955), pp. 444–449. Honor was not restricted to those of high birth, but could also be the possession of a peasant.

STURGIS E. LEAVITT, "Pedro Crespo and the Captain in Calderón's *El alcalde de Zalamea," Hispania,* XXXVIII (1955), pp. 430–431. Calderón provides some good lines to the actor who plays

Crespo. He also tries to direct the sympathy of the audience to the right character.

C. A. SOONS, "Caracteres e imágenes en *El alcalde de Zalamea*," *Romanische Forschungen*, LXXII (1960), pp. 104–107. Shows how honor is closely related to prudence.

Jealousy, the Greatest Monster (*El mayor monstruo los celos*)

EVERETT W. HESSE, "Obsesiones en *El mayor monstruo del mundo* de Calderón," *Estudios*, VIII, No. 23 (mayo-agosto, 1952), pp. 395–409. All the characters are motivated by obsessions that make them lose something of their human qualities and hurl them into the realm of the abstract.

——— "El arte calderoniano en *El mayor monstruo los celos*," *Clavileño*, VII, No. 38 (marzo-abril, 1956), pp. 18–30. The play is a fusion of traditional elements derived principally from Seneca and Aristotle.

Life is a Dream (*La vida es sueño*)

ARTURO FARINELLI, *La vita è un sogno*, 2 vols. (Turin: Fratelli Bocca, 1916). A monumental work tracing the sources of the idea that life is a dream.

EVERETT W. HESSE, "La concepción calderoniana del príncipe perfecto en *La vida es sueño*," *Clavileño*, IV, No. 20 (marzo-abril, 1953), pp. 4–12. Traces the concept of the perfect prince to Thomistic philosophy.

FELIX G. OLMEDO, *Las fuentes de "La vida es sueño": La idea, el cuento, el drama*, (Madrid: Editorial Voluntad, 1928). A brief account of the sources of the notion that life is a dream.

MICHELE FEDERICO SCIACCA, "Verdad y sueño de *La vida es sueño* de Calderón de la Barca," *Clavileño*, I, No. 2 (marzo-abril, 1950), pp. 1–9. The only thing not a dream for Segismundo was the beauty of Rosaura.

ALBERT E. SLOMAN, "The Structure of Calderón's *La vida es sueño*," *Modern Language Review*, XLVIII (1953), pp. 293–300. Distinguishes two plots: the first concerns Segismundo's conversion, and the second the restoration of Rosaura's honor.

WILLIAM M. WHITBY, "Rosaura's Role in the Structure of *La vida es sueño*," *Hispanic Review*, XXVIII (1960), pp. 16–27. Explains in detail Rosaura's part in the conversion of Segismundo.

E. M. WILSON, "*La vida es sueño*," *Revista de la Universidad de Buenos Aires*, Tercera época, IV, Nos. 3 y 4 (1946), pp. 61–78. An exaggerated pride and excessive self-confidence bring about the disillusion and subsequent awakening or downfall of all the characters except Rosaura and Clotaldo. Considers the secondary plot an integral part of the main action.

The Wonder-Working Magician (*El mágico prodigioso*)

WILLIAM J. ENTWISTLE, "Justina's Temptation: An Approach to the Understanding of Calderón," *Modern Language Review*, XL (1945), pp. 180–189. Analyzes the roles of free-will and despair in the temptation of Justina.

EVERETT W. HESSE, "The Function of the Romantic Action in *El mágico prodigioso*," *Bulletin of the Comediantes*, XVII, No. 1 (Spring, 1965), pp. 5–7. The theme of truth links the romantic and religious actions.

BRUCE W. WARDROPPER, "The Interplay of Wisdom and Saintliness in *El mágico prodigioso*," *Hispanic Review*, XI (1943), pp. 116–123. Following Thomistic tradition, Calderón dramatizes the interdependence of the problems posed by the two ideal Christian types, the sage and the saint.

The Devotion of the Cross (*La devoción de la cruz*)

WILLIAM J. ENTWISTLE, "Calderón's *La devoción de la cruz*," *Bulletin Hispanique*, L (1948), pp. 472–482. The symbol of the cross represents Grace which, when accepted voluntarily by the sinner, can save him from damnation, no matter how late the repentance.

EDWIN HONIG, "Calderón's Strange Mercy Plays," *Massachusetts Review* (Autumn, 1961). *The Devotion of the Cross* considered as an allegory.

The Painter of His Dishonor (*El pintor de su deshonra*)

C. A. SOONS, "El problema de los juicios estéticos en Calderón. *El pintor de su deshonra*," *Romanische Forschungen*, LXXVI (1964), pp. 155–162. The art of the work must be considered in a three-dimensional framework of measure, proportion and correspondence in regard to its language and imagery.

BRUCE W. WARDROPPER, "The Unconscious Mind in Calderón's *El pintor de su deshonra*," *Hispanic Review*, XVIII (1950), pp. 285–301. Serafina's death was not the act of cold-blooded murder but the result of a sin by the unconscious mind.

The Constant Prince (*El príncipe constante*)

CARLOS ORTIGOZA VIEYRA, *Los móviles de la comedia: "El príncipe constante" de Calderón de la Barca*, (Mexico: Robredo, 1957). Studies the sources, performances, editions and translations of the work. Concludes with an analysis of the play's motives, act by act.

ALBERT E. SLOMAN, *The Sources of Calderón's El príncipe constante,"* (Oxford: Basil Blackwell, 1950). Contains a reproduction of the play, *La fortuna adversa.*

BRUCE W. WARDROPPER, "Christian and Moor in Calderón's *El príncipe constante," Modern Language Review,* LIII (1958), pp. 512–520. Calderón modifies the literary tradition of the sentimental Moor by stressing religious rather than sentimental differences. Points out also that the reader must recognize Calderón as a dramatic poet rather than as a dramatist.

EDWARD M. WILSON AND WILLIAM J. ENTWISTLE, "Calderón's *Príncipe constante:* Two Appreciations," *Modern Language Review,* XXXIV (1939), pp. 207–222. According to Wilson, Calderón shows how a good man becomes a saint; for Entwistle the play is a great symbolic drama.

The Surgeon of His Honor (*El médico de su honra*)

BRUCE W. WARDROPPER, "Poetry and Drama in Calderón's *El médico de su honra," Romanic Review,* XLIX, (1958), pp. 3-11. The play contains its own sets of poetic images, its own rationale and is an entity unto itself. It must be read as dramatic poetry to be fully understood.

English Translations of Plays and Autos

EDWARD FITZGERALD, *Eight Dramas of Calderón.* Freely translated. (London and New York: Macmillan, 1906). The translations are abridged and give a false and distorted impression of Calderón's genius.

EDWIN HONIG, *Four Plays.* (New York: Hill and Wang, 1961). Contains *Secret Vengeance for Secret Insult; Devotion to the Cross; The Mayor of Zalamea;* and *The Phantom Lady.* Perhaps one of the best volumes of translations available.

WILLIAM E. COLFORD, *The Mayor of Zalamea.* (Great Neck, New York: Barron's Educational Series, 1959). A superior translation.

——— *Life is a Dream.* (Great Neck, New York: Barron's Educational Series, 1958). Another excellent translation.

ROY CAMPBELL, *The Surgeon of His Honour.* (Madison, Wisconsin: University of Wisconsin Press, 1960). An outstanding rendition in verse.

WILLIS KNAPP JONES, *The Feast of Belshazzar* in *Spanish One-Act Plays in English.* (Dallas: Tardy, 1934). First rate.

MACK HENDRICKS SINGLETON, *The Great Theater of the World,* in *Masterpieces of the Spanish Golden Age,* (New York: Rinehart, 1957). The best translation available of this *auto.*

Selected Bibliography

Studies on the Autos sacramentales

EUGENIO FRUTOS CORTÉS, *La filosofía de Calderón en sus autos sacramentales.* (Zaragoza: C.S.I.C., 1952). The first part is a study of Calderon's epoch and philosophical bent. The second classifies the themes of the *autos* into the Universe, Man, Life, Death and Dreams, The World as a Moral Theme, and Theme of God.

STURGIS E. LEAVITT, "Humor in the *autos* of Calderón," *Hispania,* XXXIX (1956), pp. 137–144. Takes issue with A. A. Parker in his condemnation of the Peasant; Leavitt's point is that "Calderón intended the *Labrador* to be not merely a humorous character, but one entirely sympathetic to the audience."

ALEXANDER A. PARKER, *The Allegorical Drama of Calderón. An Introduction to the Autos Sacramentales.* (Oxford and London: Dolphin, 1943). The best interpretive study of the *autos, The Great Theater of the World* (*El gran teatro del mundo*); *Belshazzar's Feast* (*La cena de Baltasar*); *Life is a Dream* (*La vida es sueño*).

A. VALBUENA PRAT, "Los autos sacramentales de Calderón: clasificación y análisis," *Revue Hispanique,* LXI (1924), pp. 1–302. A definitive study on the classification and analysis of Calderón's *autos.*

BRUCE W. WARDROPPER, "The Search for a Dramatic Formula for the *auto sacramental.*" *PMLA,* LXV (1950), pp. 1196–1211. Whereas Valdivielso develops the concept of man as an individual, Calderón deals with mankind in general. Valdivielso is an ascete-dramatist, Calderón a theologian-dramatist.

——— *Introducción al teatro religioso del Siglo de Oro.* (Madrid: Revista de Occidente, 1954). A thorough and complete account of the evolution of the *auto sacramental* from 1500 to 1648. Destroys the false impression that Calderón was the sole creator of the *auto.*

The Age of Calderón

R. TREVOR DAVIES, *The Golden Century of Spain (1501–1621).* (London and New York: Macmillan, 1937). An excellent background work, especially for the early seventeenth century.

——— *Spain in Decline (1621–1700).* (London and New York: Macmillan, 1957). Brief complement to the earlier work,

J. H. ELLIOTT, *Imperial Spain, 1469–1716.* (London: Arnold, 1963). Another background book of authoritative quality.

MARTIN HUME, *The Court of Philip IV.* (New York: Brentano, 1907). Provides the courtly background in which Calderón lived and wrote.

The Question of Honor

P. N. DUNN, "Honour and the Christian Background in Calderón," *Bulletin of Hispanic Studies,* XXXVII (1960), pp. 75–105. Calderón views honor as a rival religion by its acts of purification and self-sacrifice. Special attention is given to *The Mayor of Zalamea,* which Dunn considers a kind of ritual. An important contribution to an understanding of a complex issue.

C. A. JONES, "Spanish Honour as Historical Phenomena, Convention and Artistic Motive," *Hispanic Review,* XXXIII (1965), pp. 32–39. Honor is a device used by the dramatist not only to develop action and conflict, but also to show something of the truth concerning human behavior.

Dramatic Theory

H. J. CHAYTOR, *Dramatic Theory in Spain.* (Cambridge: University Press, 1925). Excerpts from the writings of sixteenth and seventeenth century authors concerning their ideas on drama.

BARRETT H. CLARK, *European Theories of the Drama.* (New York: Crown, 1947), pp. 83–98. Useful. Has a translation of Lope's *The New Art of Writing Plays in This Age,* as well as excerpts from the writings on dramatic theory by other well-known authors.

WILLIAM CARLTON MCCRARY, "The Classical Background of Spanish Dramatic Theory of the Sixteenth and Seventeenth Centuries." Unpublished doctoral dissertation. (University of Wisconsin, 1958). The major dramatists and dramatic critics believed they were reinterpreting the ideas of Aristotle or Horace or adjusting these ideas to meet their own needs. Spanish dramatic theory is viewed as evolutionary rather than revolutionary.

Studies on Golden Age Drama and Theater

STURGIS E. LEAVITT, "The Popular Appeal of Golden Age Drama in Spain," *University of North Carolina Extension Bulletin,* XXVIII, No. 3 (1949), pp. 7–15. Audiences sought an afternoon's diversion and the *comedia* provided action, love interest, conflict, honor, national heroes and Spanish traditions.

A. A. PARKER, *The Approach to the Spanish Drama of the Golden Age.* (London: The Hispanic and Luso-Brazilian Councils, 1957). Reprinted in *Tulane Drama Review* (Autumn, 1959), pp. 42–59. Sets forth five principles for an understanding of the structure of the *comedia.*

——— "Reflections on a New Definition of Baroque," *Bulletin of*

Hispanic Studies, XXX (1953), pp. 142–151. The technical maturity of the Spanish *comedia* is marked by the unification of dramatic themes and coherence of dramatic structure, influenced by the Classical esthetic. Parker takes issue with Roaten and Sánchez y Escribano's dichotomy of "Renaissance" and "Baroque" drama and their attempts to define Spanish drama in terms of plastic arts.

ARNOLD G. REICHENBERGER, "The Uniqueness of the *Comedia,*" *Hispanic Review,* XXVII (1959), pp. 303–316. The *comedia* has its own laws, structure and imagery and is an expression of the ideals of a people.

HUGO A. RENNERT, *The Spanish Stage in the Time of Lope de Vega.* (New York: Hispanic Society of America, 1909). Invaluable for the staging of the *comedia,* lives of famous actors and actresses of the period, and a description of the early theaters. Reprinted in 1963 by Dover Publications (New York), with the omission of the original edition's list of actors and actresses.

DARNELL H. ROATEN AND F. SÁNCHEZ Y ESCRIBANO, *Wölfflin's Principles in Spanish Drama: 1500–1700,* (New York: Hispanic Institute in the United States, 1952). Wölfflin's principles are translated into terms appropriate to another medium to provide a basis for the judgment of all other Spanish literary forms. Baroque drama adheres to an ideal of beauty characteristic of the epoch.

GERALD E. WADE, "Interpretation of the *comedia,*" *Bulletin of the Comediantes,* XI (Spring, 1959), pp. 1–6. Contends that it is impossible to determine definitively what a play meant to a Golden Age dramatist because every work of literature means different things to different peoples in different epochs.

Index

Index